Winter in America

by

August Sommers

1

Our First Date

It was the summer I'd just graduated college when I returned to New York and everything was grand. It had only taken me three and a half years and I was back in the place I loved best. New York was alive and vibrant back in '84.

A man once told me to take any city in the U.S. and times it by ten and there you had New York City. He didn't have to tell me. It moved at another speed. It was like a city on steroids and I loved it. The opportunities were there if I just played my cards right but right now what I needed was a job.

Pops must have read my thoughts and steered me to a position at Medgar Evers University in Brooklyn where he was chairman of their entering college freshman program. Many of the entering college freshmen needed some type of remedial help so I was hired on as a remedial writing tutor.

Both parents having taught I was born with a genetic chromosome to teach or so I was programmed to think. So, tutoring these entering college freshman was welcomed by me.

My father making sure I understood the basic tenets of my new job assigned me to his classroom. I'd grown up observing my father in a classroom so this was not new to me. And because I thought my father to be a brilliant man who I had been estranged from while doing a brief stint in the military and college I also welcomed being close to my father again whether commuting or hanging out in the newly revitalized Brooklyn at the Jamaican Day Parade or at one of Brooklyn's open mic. But what I most enjoyed was being in the classroom and watching him teach. He was a masterful teacher. He had such a quiet and unassuming approach to teaching that he made it a pleasant occasion each time you'd step into his classroom and it hardly mattered whether or not they exited as the next John Oliver Killens or Ralph Ellison they'd all taken tremendous strides towards realizing their potential. He made sure of that and their gratitude showed.

The day prior to my starting he asked me to remain at the table following dinner.

"You excited about starting work tomorrow?"

"I think I'm more nervous than excited," I said a little puzzled by his question.

"That's understandable. Just remember to keep your nose clean and stay professional. There are a lot of pretty ladies there but remember you never work and play in the same place. Keep that in mind."

I understood an also knew that any indiscretion and they would not look at the professor's son but at the Chairman of the English Department. Still, I was on a career path that would have me in my own classroom when school started in the fall and I had a lady who was planning to move up here to be close to me so he didn't know that as right as he was I wasn't interested in women at this time.

What I didn't realize at twenty eight was that you didn't have to be interested in women to be swept off your feet by one. And that's exactly what happened when I first laid eyes on Tina. I was literally shaken to my foundation. Standing on the shy side of five feet this little bustling ball of brown energy was just as cute as she was vivacious. We flirted continuously until I garnered the courage to get her phone number. After that we talked endlessly on the phone at night and I couldn't wait to be in her company the following morning.

I told her of my father's rules and she told me of her two year old daughter. Every now and then she'd pulled me away from school and we'd end up by Ebbet's Field where I'd steal a kiss. This went on for the better part of a month and a half until the last week of school when we went, as part of a class trip to the Fulton Fish Market in lower Manhattan. It was a good time for all and it was the first time we openly showed our affections in public although most of the class of women seemed to already know. Summer school ended that week and I asked her out to dinner that Friday. We were to meet at her house in Bed-Stuy.

I arrived for my date dressed in my hardest New York b-boy attire for my date with Tina only to find she wasn't home. I'd travelled two hours after waiting a month to see her and wasn't about to be denied. There were no cell phones back then so I had a seat on the stoop to wait. We'd both waited patiently for the semester to end so we could share each other's company she maybe more than I so I knew there had to be something wrong as time moved on.

Fact-of-the-matter was she was a nice girl, quiet and assuming with a soft-spoken nature that only endeared her to others. Me. Well there was no question I was either falling in love with her or I'd already done so and hadn't realized it yet.

"Hey baby," she said grinning widely as we hugged.

"You had me worried."

"Didn't mean to. I had an asthma attack because of the heat and I went to my doctors to get my asthma medication," she said holding up the bag. "You been here long?" she asked brushing by me and entering the brownstone and heading down the basement stairs.

Tina had a tiny room in the basement with a single bed and a TV which sat on an old, gray, fold up chair in the corner.

I felt comfortable with her sitting on the bed next to me even though it was our first time alone. Good conversation and her easy laugh made it right as rain and we were soon sweating, trying to catch our breath while still entwined in each other's bodies.

I was spent and happy. We'd made it past another hurdle. She'd been everything she promised and my heart soared with all of the possibilities for the two of us. I'd marry her and adopt the baby. I'd been thinking about it even though I hadn't dated her yet. It was just that good and tonight confirmed our compatibility so what else could there be. Still, I'm going to wait and do it right.

"Malik please get my pills off the kitchen counter?"Tina said coughing and trying to catch her breath.

I did as I was told and returned immediately with the pills which I handed her before realizing that she was going to need some water to take the pills. When I returned this time the pills were all over the floor.

"Call an ambulance!" she shouted at me.

I took the stairs two-by-two and rushed across the street and called 911 before rushing back down the steps and helping her upstairs and to the stoop.

Now I know you always hear about it being easier to hail a cab than to wait on an ambulance in the ghetto but it was only minutes before the ambulance pulled up taking the weight of the world off my hands.

"I want to walk Malik," Tina said to me. So, while the ambulance drivers were securing their equipment I walked my baby from the stoop to the front gate and back again countless times all the while talking to her.

"Just have a seat sir. We'll be with you momentarily. We seem to have locked the oxygen tube and mask in the ambulance. We've called another ambulance and we're just waiting for them to arrive. Why don't you and your lady friend just have a seat until they arrive?"

Thinking he knew best I had Tina sit on my lap to wait. She wasn't really responding to anything I was saying right through here and I wondered how she was feeling. Was my baby hurting? What could I do? Did she know I had plans on marrying her? And it was then, at that very moment that I heard her teeth grinding together and cracking and felt my pants leg become wet with urine. And there Tina died in my lap on our first date.

Mattie Green

The walk from the subway seemed longer than usual. The crows feet growing from the corners of her eyes grew longer and more pronounced as she approached the young men on the corner of 150th and 8th plying their trade. Her first thoughts were to cross over but after being on her feet since six this morning she had neither the energy nor the desire to take another step. All she wanted to do at this point was to get to her tiny Dunbar apartment wash the smell of the subway off, grab a quick bite and get in her bed. She was exhausted to say the least. She couldn't remember the last time she hadn't been tired. At thirty eight she felt sixty. She only hoped her seventeen year old, Jazmine had fixed dinner.

Getting closer to the small group of young men she relaxed recognizing most as Tayshawn's little posse. Tayshawn, now eighteen, and her oldest had grown up with most of the boys and still regarded them as friends although she wished he had chosen a better group. It wasn't that they were bad boys but circumstances being what they were didn't allow them many choices and even with choices they had no one to push them to do anything other than what they were doing.

"Evening Ms.Greene,"Abdul said smiling. "Need some help with those bags?"

"No. Thank you. I'm good,"

Kilo and Sherrod nodded and spoke as well.

"You boys seen Tayshawn?"

"I think he's in the bodega getting something to drink. Want me to get him for you?" Sherrod asked.

"If you wouldn't mind," Mattie said placing the bags of groceries down gently on the concrete sidewalk. "Hope y'all ain't out here doin' anything you ain't s'pozed to be doin'."

"Ah, no ma'am. C'mon Ms. Greene. How long have you known me?" Abdul said smiling.

"Known you since you was just a pup. Used to change your diapers. Know your mother too. Know her well," Mattie said sending the teen a threatening glance. "And know that big as you are she'd come down here and snatch your butt up if she knew you were out here selling that poison."

"You right!" Abdul said grinning widely now. "But you know I don't sell no poison. C'mon Ms. Greene. Have you ever known me to do anything illegal? I've never been in trouble in my life and ain't going to start now."

"I certainly hope not. You know I'm keeping my eye on you Abdul. I look at all of you as mine and I don't want anything to happen to you out here in these streets," Mattie said turning to make sure she made eye contact with all the boys.

"I hear you and appreciate that Ms. Greene," Abdul said staring down at the pavement now.

"Hey ma," Tayshawn said walking up and kissing the smallish woman on the cheek and grabbing the bags of groceries.

"Be right back son," he said to Abdul his lifelong friend.

"How was your day ma?"

"No different. Same as usual. And yours? Did you call or go down to John Jay?"

"You'll be happy to know that I did. Turned in my high school transcripts along with the application and applied for financial aid. Do you know that it cost me thirty dollars just to file the application?"

"Welcome to the real world, Tay. That's a pretty cheap investment on your future. That thirty dollars is the first steps to you earning six figures. So, did they tell you when you'd hear from them?"

"They said seven to ten days but you already know. With my high school transcripts and S.A.T scores I could have gone anywhere. I really should have gone to Columbia and it would have been closer but I don't want to be taxed yet. I'll go there to get my masters or my law degree. But right now I've got too much else going on," he said grinning at his mother.

"And I hope it's not slingin' on the corner with your so-called friends," Mattie said staring at the young man that towered over her at six foot four and a half.

"C'mon ma. When have you ever known for me to do anything but the right thing?"

"Where did you get the application fee?"

"I stopped by the barbershop and told daddy I need the application fee. He was only too glad to give it to me. Told me he wished he hadn't been so quick to make a buck and had gone to college. Gave me the old lecture about not wanting to be on my feet at forty."

Mattie Green smiled. If there was one thing she had to be proud of it was her children. Tayshawn who had been a hellion in elementary and middle school had miraculously turned it around and managed to climb to the top of his high school class upon graduation. She had never been so proud and Jazmine was intent on besting all that Tayshawn had done.

Sticking the key in the door she pulled her oldest down and kissed him on the cheek.

"What was that for?"

"That's for making me proud to have a son as beautiful as you."

"Does that mean you can lend me a twenty?"

"Boy what do I look like First National Bank?"

"Okay. How about fifteen?"

"Goodness, Tay can you let mommy get in the house good? Hey mommy. How was your day?"

"Good. Tiring but I made it so I guess I'm good. And yours?"

"Got an 'A' on Ms. Jackson's English paper."

"I'm proud of you although I wouldn't expect anything less from you. Is that the same Ms. Jackson that gave Tay such a hard time last year?"

"That's her. The very same. The woman's no joke. She says that if we do well in her course college will seem like a breeze. I believe her too. In twelve years of school I have never worked so hard. She's like a drill sergeant. You know Kylie. She came in and handed her her project and it wasn't in the right kind of folder and she rejected it. It didn't matter that Kylie spent two weeks writing it. She didn't even bother to look at it she just saw the folder and rejected it. The woman's a trip."

"She's just preparing you for the real world. She's good for you. You can't cut corners and take short cuts," Mattie said to her daughter as she took off the worn, white blouse she wore everyday as part of her maids uniform. Still as crisp and white as the day she first donned it she threw it into the dirty clothes pile in the corner of her tiny bedroom. Pulling the curtains back she gazed onto 8th Avenue below and saw Abdul and Kilo pandering to customers as they came up the subway stairs. Mattie counted four sales in only a matter of minutes.

16

'Lying little heathens,' she remarked to herself before lowering her bra straps revealing the red marks. Rubbing the marks she promised she'd buy herself a new bra when she got paid as she'd done the past five years but something always came up to prevent her and now that she'd gained a pound or two the bra cut deeply into her shoulders and back. And it would cut into her for another two weeks before she'd let Tayshawn get out there with Abdul and the rest of his crew and throw away his future. He never asked for much seemingly satisfied to wear last year's clothes and to just do without rather than to get out there and shame her or jeopardize his future. In these times when so many like Tay were out there just like her Tay she knew she was blessed. Abdul came from the same type of home and Lord knows Ms. Gibson loved that boy to death but there he was.

"Mattie I'm going out. Don't wait up for me."

Hearing Tayshawn's voice she had to smile. Ever since she'd told him how the white kids down on Park Avenue acted showing their parents no respect and referring them by their first names Tayshawn teased her calling her Matilda or Mattie. The first time she'd taken the broom and beaten him to the floor both laughing until the tears rolled down their cheeks. Now it had become a running joke and when he sensed his mother was down he would pull out all the stops and then go running from what she would do next.

"Mattie. Do you hear me talking to you?"

Mattie smiled but didn't answer sitting down, the pile of bills in front of her. Doling out a few dollars to each she finished with forty eight dollars left over. Putting on the old weather beaten rag she called a robe she opened the door and made her way to the living room where she plopped into her favorite recliner the stack of bills on her lap.

"You ready to eat mama?" Jazmine asked pulling the hairnet down over her hair as she readied herself for work.

"When you are sweetheart. What's for dinner?"

"The usual. Baked chicken, mashed potatoes and a salad but I don't have time to eat. I'm running late as it is. I'll grab a sandwich or something at work."

"Girl you're going to dry up and blow away if you don't stop running and start eating," Mattie said to her favorite and only daughter who weighed all of a hundred pounds dripping wet. "Where's your brother?"

"Where else? In his bedroom chomping at the bit waiting for you to give him that early release so he can get back to his thug friends." Jazzy said handing her mother the plate.

"Let me ask you something Jazz. I know you and your brother are tight and I don't want you to say anything if it means betraying his trust but he's not out there selling drugs with Abdul and Sherrod is he?"

Jazz was shocked at her mother's question but couldn't help bursting out in laughter.

"Tay?" she said as if her mother had lost her mind. "C'mon mommy. You see the way that poor boy dresses and the way the rest of his crew dresses. Tay ain't slingin' or blingin'. Everybody on the block knows he's as straight as they come. I mean those have been his friends since they were little playin' cops and niggas but when they chose that rode he wasn't with it.

He's always wanted to be a lawyer and one day he'll be representing his boys. It's sad to say 'cause for the most part they're all pretty much the same. They're not all hard and rough— well except for Kilo—he's already been to Rikers a couple of times but that's because he basically raised himself. I can't believe you asked me that. I thought you knew your own son better than that."

""I'd like to think that I do but I wouldn't think that Abdul and Sherrod would be out there either," Mattie replied.

"They grew up differently than Tay did mama. Yeah, his mom works hard too but it's different. When you come home, no matter how tired you were it was always, 'How was school today Tay? How are you doing in Ms. Jackson's class? Did you finish your paper? Let me see it. And then you would read it and sit down with him and go over it with him. And believe me he saw that. He used to ask me if I thought Abdul's mother really loved him because she didn't treat him the way he thought a parent was supposed to treat a kid. He was comparing his mother to you. That's all it was."

Mattie felt a warm feeling go through her. She didn't feel nearly as tired as she did when she'd first come in the door.

"Thanks daughter."

"No problem mother," the girl said smiling. "Glad to be of some help. I get off at ten and it's payday so ask Tay to meet me at the train station at ten twenty," the teenager said buttoning her parka and heading out the door.

"Be safe, baby."

"Always," Jazzy replied locking the door behind her.

"Tay!" Mattie screamed.

The young man came at the sound of his mother's voice.

"Yeah, ma. I guess I dozed off."

"Yeah, I guess standing on the corner all day will wear you out."

"It does take its toll on you. Seriously though ma, after going down to the college I walked all over the city and I don't know if I'm paranoid or not but it just seems like no one wants to hire me. I don't know if it's because I just graduated from high school and don't have any experience or because I'm Black."

"Chances are it's a little bit of both but believe me it's hard out there for everybody. I was talking to your aunt and she was telling me that she has college grads coming in with resumes from the most prestigious colleges and all the experience in the world and they can't find a job. The job market is tough right through here even though Obama says it's on the upswing. But don't get discouraged. Persistence overcomes resistance. It'll work out for you Tay. Just hang in there."

"I will ma," Tay responded. "Do you mind if I go out for awhile?"

"I don't have a problem with you going out. But I want to show you something before you leave and perhaps you can explain something to me."

"Sure. What is it?"

Mattie got up and grabbed her son by the hand and led him into her bedroom.

"What's up ma?"

Mattie pulled back the shades and pointed to the four young men on the street below.

"Please tell me who that is?"

Tay gazed out the window.

"You know who that is, ma."

"Tell me."

"Abdul, Kilo and Sherrod. I don't know the other kid," he said nonchalantly.

"That's what I thought. And what is it that they're doing?"

"I don't know what you mean ma."

"I just want you to explain to me what activity they're engaged in? I'm having a hard time trying to understand why strangers are continually approaching them."

"You know what they're doing, ma." Tay said smiling sheepishly.

"Yes I do. Those are your friends out there selling poison and killing Black folks, killing family members. And you're okay with that?"

"C'mon ma. You know I don't get down like that."

"But you associate with them and when the police do a raid they're not going to see Tayshawn the college student. They're not going to see anything but a nigga out there slingin'."

"You're right ma. But you know that no matter where I am or what I do I'll always be a nigga in the police's eyes."

Mattie dropped her head. She knew Tay was right but…

"I hear you baby but you can lessen your chances of being picked up."

"Like Trayvon, Eric Garner and Mike Brown? What was there crime? None of them were standing on the corner. There only crime was being Black. And that's one thing I can't hide from whether I'm on the corner with my friends or just catching the subway in case you haven't noticed."

"So, you condone what they're doing? You condone their killing other Black folks."

"No ma. I don't condone them selling drugs. You know that but I understand them. They just tryna eat. Kilo and Sherrod don't have no fam. They're basically on their own. Sherrod's mother's in rehab and his daddy is upstate in Sing Sing doing a ten year bid. What's the boy supposed to do? Are you going to take them in? We strugglin' as it is. Most of the people up here in Harlem are strugglin'. What they supposed to do? I just got finished tellin'

23

you how I spent all day tryna find a job. Just ain't a whole lotta opportunities out here for a nigga."

"I hear you son. And I understand. I take crap everyday from white folk who pay me barely enough to keep a roof over our heads. That's why I don't want to see my only son hemmed up. It's called guilt by association. You know what they say. Birds of a feather flock together."

"I hear you ma," Tay said anxious to end the conversation. "So what do you think I should do?"

"Just put a little distance between yourselves and your friends. In a couple of weeks you'll be entering a whole new world. You'll meet new and different people. Your circle of friends will expand exponentially. You don't have to wait for that to happen. You can make that happen."

"I hear you ma."

"Do you?"

"I do."

"Hand me my purse," Mattie said.

Tayshawn handed his mother her worn brown leather pocketbook. The C's indicating Coach were now faded and now looked like O's.

"How much did you say you needed?"

Tayshawn recognizing the gravity of his mother's words had difficulty answering.

"Whatever you can spare ma."

He knew that the little she made went into taking care of he and Jazz. And she sacrificed everything for the sake of her kids never ever spending a dime on herself and contented herself on window shopping in the Jessica London and Macy's catalogs that came in the mail. All this so they could have a better life than they had now.

She pulled the crumpled twenty out of her purse and handed it to him. He thanked her and pulled the door closed behind him and headed to his room.

"Tayshawn."

"Yeah ma."

"What are your plans for the night?"

"Well I was going to ask you if it was okay if I took Desiree to the movies."

"I guess that would be fine. What are you going to see?"

"Well, she really wants to see Selma so I guess Selma it is."

"Smart girl and from what I hear it's supposed to be a good movie and entertaining too. I always did like her. Has she decided where she's going to college this fall?"

"No ma'am. She's still undecided but deep down she really wants to go to Brown or Columbia but that all depends on what type of scholarships and grants she gets. But even with them she's still going to need financial aid. I think she's leaning towards Columbia though. She wants to stay close to home for obvious reasons," he smiled.

"And those are?"

"C'mon ma," he said his smile growing larger now. "You know she can't be too far from Mattie's boy."

"Get outta here boy!" Mattie said grinning widely.

"Thanks ma" Tay said his tone and face returning to deep thought and reflection. "I want you to know that I head every word you said and I hear you. You'd probably be surprised to know that I tell the fellas the same thing you were telling me about destroying our community by selling that poison."

"And what do they say?"

"The same thing I was telling you. Kilo usually says 'yeah I don't come from a home like you do bro. Ain't no Ms. Greene putting no food on the table for me, son. Nigga gotta eat.'

And being that he's all he's got I understand but Abdul's the one that really gets me because he comes from a loving family and has both his mom and pops and they provide for him and he's got a nice crib and everything. I think he just likes the game and all that goes along with it like the clothes and the chicks but he doesn't have to do it. When it's just the two of us, like today when he went downtown with me to enroll in school and I ask him why he does it he just says, 'What you gone and did; sign up for the Nation of Islam' or he calls me little Malcolm and laughs. But I get where you're coming from. I don't mess around though. I just hang around cause I grew up with them and they're the only friends I got."

"I understand. And as long as you and I understand I'm okay with that but don't let your friends get you caught up. They're not your friends if they do. And I've worked too hard and too long trying to provide a better future than was afforded me. You're right on the cusp of doing great things so don't blow it son."

"I won't ma," he said bending over and kissing his mother on the cheek.

"I almost forgot. Mattie asked me to ask you if you could pick her up at ten thirty when she gets off at the subway station."

"Well, so much for the movies," Tay said shrugging his shoulders. "I guess Dez and me can go to the matinee tomorrow and make a day of it. Saturday's probably better anyway.

Today is payday and these fools be out there robbing and shootin'. Yeah Saturday's probably better anyway. Do you mind if she comes over and just hangs out then?"

"I'd like that," Mattie said smiling glad that her son recognized the dangers that were out there.

"Okay but just remember she's comin' to see me ma so don't be hoggin'up all the conversation," Tay said pulling out his cell phone. "Sometimes I think that girl likes you more than she likes me."

"Can you blame her? Why take a replica when you can have the real thing?"

"Yeah. Okay Mattie. Whatever you say."

"You're going to stop calling me by first name," she said jumping up and running to grab the broom, skillet or whatever she could get her hands on.

An hour later, the three sat in the living room watching a bootleg copy of John Wick one of Mattie's clients at work had burned for her. At somewhere around ten fifteen Tay paused the movie.

"C'mon Dez. I gotta go pick up Jazz."

"Just when it was getting good," Mattie commented.

"We'll be right back ma."

The two walked downstairs and crossed the busy boulevard.

"If a nigga can't make a grand a night something's wrong," Abdul boasted serving one customer as two stood in line. Kilo and Sherrod were equally as busy filling requests and hardly noticed Tay and Dez passing in the busy Friday night crowd.

"What up son?" Abdul said catching Tay out of the corner of his eye.

"You the man," he responded nonchalantly as he thought about the conversation he had not too long ago with his mother. A young teenage with a baby carriage stood in the long procession waiting to be served and Tay wondered what kind of life the baby would have with a mother strung out on dope. Yeah, ma was right. These were Black folks killing each other for a few trinkets and some chump change. Tay's stomach turned.

"I was wondering where your ass was son. You need to come get some of this," Abdul said holding up the thick roll of twenties. It was early and they were pumping.

"I'll pass, son," Tay responded.

"It's M.O.B. Money over bitches you henpecked motherfucker," he heard Kilo say.

"Who you calling a bitch?" Dez said turning to Kilo.

Tay glanced back up at the fourth floor window and saw his mother standing watching. He knew he was in her prayers and pulled Dez along.

"C'mon Dez. Don't pay that stupid motherfucker no mind."

Minutes later they saw Jazz coming up the subway stairs. The girls greeted each other warmly and for most of the walk home Tay was speechless. It was unusual for young teenage girls to get along so well but the two did and chatted constantly even when he wasn't around. At first Tay thought Dez was checking up on him when she would call Jazz but after two years it was apparent that the two genuinely liked each other. Often times now he felt like he was the intruder.

Five minutes later only a few feet from where they had been they were engulfed in blue and red lights. The 33d Precinct was out in full force. Approaching the scene he saw his mother standing in front of his building looking on at the growing crowd of onlookers.

Willie, one of the neighborhood kids rode up to Tay on his bike.

"What's up son," Tay asked as he grabbed the girls and crossed over 8th to avoid the crowd and the cops.

"I don't know Tay. All I know is somebody got shot," he said before speeding away.

"Ma?"

Mattie Greene looked more exhausted than usual. She grabbed Tay and hugged him as if her life depended on it before staring up at him. The words came slowly.

"From what the cops are saying it was an apparent robbery. Abdul and Sherrod are dead."

Mattie's Confession

Mattie reached over and turned off the clock radio. She wanted to take it and throw it but thought better and swung her thick chocolate legs over the side other full sized bed. There was little space between the bed and the vanity and she wondered if she would ever do any better than this glorified closet. Well, she certainly wouldn't if she didn't get herself together and get her behind to work.

Walking the five steps to the kitchen she heard the front door slam. Tay had found a little place down in the East Village and Jazz was finishing up her senior year in high school and had already been accepted into Hofstra. The house was so quiet without Tay and soon Jazz would be gone as well. For Mattie it was time to reassess her life. She was paying a little over two thousand dollars a month for the tiny two bedroom hovel they had the nerve to call an apartment.

It was time to make a move. Her kids grown now she neither needed the space or that damn job. When their father, Quadir left right after Jazz was born she was forced to take the first job that she could find to support her kids. The fact that it was as a domestic down on Park Avenue hardly mattered. She could feed her kids but now after twenty one years working for the Hansboroughs it was time to think about Mattie.

Mattie donned the black and white maids' uniform and stepped out into the brisk March air. She had a little money saved and today she would give Mr. Hansborough her two weeks' notice. Mattie had been giving her two week's notice for close to twenty years now but with Jazz leaving on a full scholarship it was time. She'd already planned on going to D.C. to stay with her sister for a month at which time she'd search for a job and an apartment. But that was jumping the gun. Today she had one item on her agenda and that was to give her two weeks' notice.

"Morning Raul," Mattie said to the Puerto Rican doorman who'd been there nearly as long as she had.

"Morning Ms. Mattie. You're looking quite chipper today," Raul said smiling and holding the door for her. The two had become fast friends over the years and he was constantly telling her that she could do better. "You want to share with me?"

"I will. Let me see how things go first. I don't want to jinx myself. I'll tell you when I get off this evening."

"I'm gonna hold you to that."

"I know you will," Mattie smiled.

Mattie used her key and stepped into the plush Park Avenue apartment at seven fifty five. In twenty one years she had yet to be late and today was no exception.

"Morning Mattie," Mr. Hansborough said not bothering to look in her direction.

"Morning Mr. Hansborough. Will you be in your office this morning?"

"Yes, I will. I'll be there until twelve. Then I have to run downtown. I have a luncheon and a meeting with some realtors from J.P. Morgan at one. Why do you ask?"

"I was wondering if you could spare a few minutes when you get a chance this morning," Mattie said as she hung up the worn, gray, woolen coat and hat in the hall closet.

Mr. Hansborough paused long enough to check the Windsor knot in his tie.

"Something bothering you Mattie?"

"No, not really. Just some concerns I've been having."

"Is it that son of mine again?" Mr. Hansborough screamed. "Damn him. I'll put his ass out if he's up to his old shit again."

Mattie smiled.

"No. No. No. J.J.'s fine Mr. Hansborough. It's nothing like that. In fact everything's fine. We just need to talk is all."

A few years back when their eldest J.J. returned from college he'd been certain he was in love with Mattie. Sincere in his thoughts he'd corner Mattie every chance he got and beg her to marry him. When she declined citing the difference in age and backgrounds he'd pout for a few days only to rebound with a new strategy. He'd even come into her bedroom on occasion after dark with the thoughts of sleeping with her. This occurred until Mattie had a face-to-face with J.J. and Mr. Hansborough but not even that stopped his approaches. It wasn't until a year or so later when he followed Mattie home and some of Tayshawn's boys took him into an alley and had a long talk with him did he stop harassing Mattie. That had been years ago but Mr. Hansborough hardly knew what was going on in his own household.

Mr. Hansborough was a good man even if he had never taken the time for anything other than the business of making money. This is one of the reasons the house always seemed to be in a state of chaos and half-a-heartbeat from World War III on a good day.

Mrs. Hansborough was the complete opposite of her husband. A traditional southern belle Jody Hansborough was content to sip Mint Juleps all day on the veranda and host supper guests as long as there was a good bottle of gin to help her through the evening. She'd grown out on the island in Wyandanch or somewhere akin and had never been further south than White Plains but she was a traditional southern wife in every sense of the word. I believe they now refer to them as trophy wives. Adept at small talk and the like but if the conversation made its way to politics or the State of the Union Address she was gone with the wind.

Missy, their youngest and only daughter was twenty one and so proper it hurt. Spoiled and brash Mattie had long ago made it a point to avoid the girl and spent a good deal of her employ ducking the blonde monster. By now she'd blossomed from a spoiled brat to a rabid Republican Tea Partier who hated anyone and everyone who wasn't rich, white and didn't have a traceable family crest.

"Mattie did they bring clean laundry back?"

"And good morning to you too Missy."

"Oh, sorry Mattie. Morning. You know daddy insists on giving the business to Lu Chang cause he sold him the building but they never ever have the laundry done on time. Should have left their asses working on the railroads. Damn Chinks! I don't know whoever gave them the laundry business. They advertise one day service and it takes them three. Could you call them for me Mattie?"

"Melissa! I know I didn't hear what I thought I heard. You save those racist remarks for your friends. I won't tolerate that kind of talk in my house. Lu Chang happens o be a friend of mine."

"I wasn't talking about Lu Chang specifically daddy. I was talking about the Chinese in general. And what have they brought to this country. Nothing but restaurants and laundries and they can't even do clothes."

Mr. Hansborough ignored the girl's remarks and headed for his study.

"Mattie would you do me a favor and see if Mrs. Hansborough needs anything and while you're up there see if J.J. has left yet. If he's still here remind him that he has a ten o'clock appointment with Bigelow & Brown to do the closing on the Soho property. When you get finished we can meet around our concerns," he said closing the door to his study grateful to have Mattie as his go between.

At fifty six he had a lot to be thankful for. He'd amassed a small fortune over the last twenty years and rivaled all but the largest realtors in Manhattan. But his home life was in shambles. His wife was for all intents and purposes no more than a nonfunctioning alcoholic who had been in and out of the Betty Ford Clinic more times than he had fingers and toes. And J.J. though quite astute with a business savvy that usurped his own simply did not possess the drive needed to take over the family business. And Missy. Well Missy was just Missy. Never too bright she adorned the page of every gossip column in all the local tabloids for her asinine antics. Her latest intrigue was as a spokesperson for the Tea Party in much the way Sarah Palin is much to their chagrin. Mr. Hansborough was by far the most level headed in Mattie's eyes but then it was difficult to maintain one's sanity in an insane asylum full of lunatics. And here Mattie found her niche though painstakingly for well over twenty years.

Knocking twice, Mattie took a deep breath and held it before entering Ms. Hansborough's boudoir. She seldom but ever left her sanctuary taking her meals here unless summoned by Mr. Hansborough to entertain guests on occasion.

"What the hell do you want? Did Henry send you up here to see if I'm sleep before he sticks his little pink pecker up in you? Is that it? Or is it my son you're sleeping with this week you little tramp?" she said before taking the latest issue of Harper's Bazaar and tossing it at Mattie's head.

"And good morning to you too Ms. Hansborough," Mattie said before easing back out the door.

"Bring me a cherry martini bitch. Shaken not stirred!" the woman screamed.

Mattie smiled and went to the mobile bar at the end of the hall and poured the woman her morning highball adding triple the vodka. It had become her morning ritual and was the only guarantee that Mattie would have a peaceful day. The triple shot of vodka would assure Mattie that the woman would sleep well into the afternoon. By then Mattie would have her cleaning and chores done and with a stiff pick me up at around three she would be out again. By the time she would awake again Mattie would be long gone.

Checking J.J.'s room she found him to be long gone and the room in impeccable shape. In all honesty J.J. may have been the least of her worries and aside from him being in love with her he presented the least problem of all.

Mattie knocked again.

"Just put it down," Ms. Hansborough screamed. And then knowing it was her last day she smiled and said.

"You want me to call Dr.Reinsdorf and see if I can't have you committed? I mean admitted."

"Why you smart little nigga bitch! You just want me gone so you can inherit my family. I know what you're up to nigga. Henry! Henry!"

Mattie quickly exited the room only to find Henry Hansborough standing at the bottom of the spiral staircase.

"She okay Mattie?" he asked his concern readily apparent.

"I'm not thinking she is. May be time to make that phone call Mr. Hansborough."

"I'm inclined to agree with you but Dr. Reinsdorf is out of the country for the next couple of weeks and I would just hate for her to try and adjust to another doctor."

"I'd hate for another doctor to have to try and adjust to her."

"Mattie. Is that anyway to speak about Ms. Hansborough?"

"Sorry sir," Mattie said out of respect for the man she had come to know so well.

"If you could just keep a close eye on her for the next couple of days I'd really appreciate it Mattie. I'm going to see if I can get in touch with Dr. Rensdorf's office and see if they can't recommend somebody until he gets back in town."

How many times had she heard that? A closer eye just meant so many more nigga bitches and no matter how much they paid her they could not pay for the abuse. And Jody Hansborough was a virtual abuse factory.

"Was J.J. in his room?"

"No sir."

"Well that's good. Maybe he's starting to take some initiative."

"If I may sir."

"Go ahead Mattie."

"J.J.'s a good boy. He's bright as a whip too. And whether you know it or not you're his idol. If you just let up on him some and didn't push him so much I think you'd be very surprised at the results."

"You don't say. And what gives you the authority to know so much about my son?"

"I have a son of my own. And growing up he didn't have half the resources that J.J. had but they're very similar in some regards. Both are bright and inquisitive. You plant the seed and they'll do the rest. My son is in Columbia Law School on a four year academic scholarship. All I did was plant the seed and have the ultimate faith in him. That's all you need."

"I'll take that into consideration Mattie. Now what is it that you wanted to talk to me about? You said you had some concerns."

"Yes sir, Mr. Hansborough. I don't know whether you realize it or not but I've been in your employ for going on twenty one years now. Every morning I've gotten up and donned this uniform and ridden the train down here to wait on and serve your family. And in those twenty one years I've never been late for work and have done what in my estimation is more than an adequate job," Mattie said pausing to catch her breath and fight back the tears.

"Adequate? You've been much more than adequate. In all honesty you've been superb. This family wouldn't have made it without you. But go ahead."

"Anyway in those twenty one years I have never received a raise."

"What? Are you serious? You know I don't handle the domestic affairs. Mrs. Hansborough is responsible for…" he said catching himself as he thought about what it was he was about to say before ending with. "I am so sorry Mattie. I will take care of that pronto," Mr. Hansborough said dropping his head embarrassed with this latest revelation.

"I'm not finished Mr. Hansborough. I want you to know I raised two kids on that meager salary and lived in a rat infested hovel for all of those twenty one years. Both of my kids received scholarships to attend college and my daughter will be leaving home in two months. For me it's a second chance at life. It's a chance to start over, to realize some of my dreams, to get out of Harlem, maybe go back to school. So, I wanted to come to you personally and give you my two week notice."

Henry Hansborough leaned back in the captains' chair and stared at Mattie for what seemed like eons when J.J. popped in.

"Well, dad I closed the deal on the Soho properties with two more over in Hackensack. Mr. Leonardi did the appraisal and says the combined value is somewhere in the neighborhood of eleven or twelve million and that's before restoration."

"Wonderful, son. Now would you give me a minute? Mattie and I are in the middle of a very important conversation."

J.J. stood there completely aghast. What could this little Black maid have that was more important than a twelve million dollar deal?

"Mattie I didn't know," was all the older man could say.

"And never once in twenty one yeas did it occur to you to inquire Mr. Hansborough. Y'all walk around here so caught up in your own lives that you don't know that other people exist. For twenty one years I was invisible except to run and fetch this or that. For twenty one years and now today I suddenly become human because the person you're so used to having do the things that you don't want to is resigning."

"Oh hell no. Get the fuck out of here! Dad! What is she saying?" J.J. interrupted.

"I know son. I feel the same way. Mattie's says she's been with us twenty one years and has never received a raise while having to raise two children in rat infested apartment off of what?"

"Two hundred and forty dollars a week," Mattie chimed in. "For twenty one years."

"Oh my God! Dad! Why didn't you give her a raise? And with all the places you own why the hell is she living under those conditions?" J.J. said his sincerity genuine as his eyes welled with tears.

"I didn't know J.J. Your mother was supposed to handle the in-house employees and their salaries."

"You can't be serious. Mattie runs the house. Mommy can't run herself. I know you're not serious," J.J. said accusingly.

"I know son. But I just assumed everything was okay and Mattie never mentioned a thing until today."

"And if you know Mattie then you should know she would never say anything. But did you ever stop to ask father? Something as simple as is everything okay with you Mattie? After all she is an integral part of the household and in any ways the most integral part. She's the one that keeps it running."

"What are you acting as her attorney now? I'm trying to wholly understand the gravity of the situation and resolve it to the best of my ability and here you are making a case against me."

"Offer her back pay and compensation then. Give her that raise and anything else she wants but we're nothing without her father and you know it."

"Thank you J.J. Now if you'll excuse us," he said offering his son the door and closing it behind him.

"The boy's right you know. And I do apologize for letting things go this long without inquiring. You know Rome wasn't built in a day but if you could just give me one day I'd like to see if I can't come up with a proposal a sort of compensation package that will sort of ease all the pain and suffering you endured while in my employ. Just give me 'til tomorrow and we can sit down and talk again. Can you do that for me?"

"I suppose I can Mr. Hansborough. I've been doin' it for twenty one years. I suppose I can do it for one more day.

Mattie held out her hand to shake sealing the deal. But Henry Hansborough wasn't having any of that at this point. He took her into his arms and hugged her tightly.

"You know J.J.'s right. You are the glue that holds this family together Mattie so... We'll meet here at nine a.m. tomorrow morning if that's good for you?"

"That's fine sir," Mattie said smiling inside.

She had no idea what Mr. H had planned for the coming day and didn't really care. She'd come to the end of the road as far as being the Hansborough's maid or anyone else's for that matter so his little compensation package was pretty much a moot point but she always remembered his advice when it came to burning bridges. Besides with this being her only job she would need him for a reference.

The rest of the day went off without a hitch. Even Ms. Hansborough was calmer than usual taking her afternoon nap after having her midday toddy. The news of Mattie's resignation hit the Hansborough household hard.

It was a funny thing though in Mattie's case. She felt more relaxed than she had in years. And the next morning felt even better. She needed the time off, the time to do some of the things she wanted to do. It was time to concentrate on all those wishes deferred.

"Good morning Raul," Mattie said tipping the doorman's hat to the back of his head and giggling like a sixteen year old.

"Wow! I missed you yesterday. You were supposed to tell me the good news," Raul said holding the door for Mattie.

"Jury's still deliberating," she said as the elevator doors closed.

"Morning Miss Mattie."

Mattie was stunned. She couldn't remember the last time Missy had addressed her as miss.

""Daddy has instructed me to tell you to keep your coat on."

"Do you know why?"

"I guess he's taking you somewhere. I don't know. Just following instructions…"

"Well, let me run up and check on your mother before I go."

"Mommy's not here. She and daddy got into it last night and I guess he got tired of her tirades and had her admitted."

"Admitted? But I thought Dr. Reinsdorf was overseas?"

"No. I think daddy hit his breaking point last night. No hospital last night. He had her admitted to Bellevue's Psychiatric Ward for long term stay. I don't think you'll have to worry about her for awhile."

"I was never worried about your mother Missy," Mattie said matter-of-factly. "But what transpired to have your father make such a drastic move."

"You know they don't let me in the loop. All I know is I came home and he was on the rampage. I was told to address you as Miss Mattie and to show you some respect or I could get the hell out and seeing how mommy was being shipped out I thought I'd best reel it in and let this play out."

Mattie smiled.

"Morning Mattie."

"Morning Mr. Hansborough."

"I'm guessing Missy told you about Ms. Hansborough."

"Just that she wasn't home."

"Oh, if I know my daughter I'm sure she did her best to fill you in," he said winking at Mattie. "Now if you'll come with me I have something that may interest you."

And with that said Henry Hansborough held the door open like the gentleman he was and led Mattie Greene downstairs and out into the crisp spring Manhattan air to the waiting limo. A few minutes later they were down in the newly renovated Soho district of the city with its quaint boutiques and million dollar hi rises. The limo pulled up and parked in front of Starbucks.

"Two Cappuccinos and an espresso."

Handing Mattie the espresso he escorted Mattie outside and down the block until they reached what appeared to be an abandoned warehouse. Mr. Hansborough rang the doorbell. Mattie was surprised when the doors slid open and J.J. greeted them.

"Dad. Ms. Mattie. Please come in."

J.J. led them in to the abandoned warehouse then down the long hall to a manual elevator. The building was old and decrepit and Mattie thought that at any minute the elevator which creaked and groaned would break down. It was soon obvious that she was not the only one having these thoughts as the elevator bumped and continued to moan.

"And you had the city inspectors come in and check everything out son."

"Yes sir and everything looks good. The first and third floors have already been rented out. I'm showing the second two a couple of prospective buyers and the fourth loft—well—who knows?"

"And this elevator?"

J.J. laughed.

"Gives the building personality. But seriously I asked the same thing on my first ride on it and the guys from Otis—you know—the elevator people assured me that all it needed was a lube job."

No sooner than J.J. said that than the elevator lurched to a stop. Mattie grabbed her stomach.

"Welcome to the loft," J.J. said ushering both his father and Mattie in before leading them on an extensive tour.

Mattie had to admit the place was gorgeous. She'd read and viewed pictures of old abandoned warehouses which were now being converted into luxury apartments and selling upwards of millions of dollars depending on their location. In the new trendy Soho district of the city this one could fetch a million easy from the pictures she'd seen in apartment and real estate magazines she browsed. She used to dream of one day owning one just like this but those dreams had long since dissipated. Still it was nice to dream.

"What do you think Mattie?" J.J. asked excitedly. "You think I can get seven hundred and fifty thou- for it?"

"Easily!"

"Do you like it," Mr. Hansborough asked.

"It's gorgeous," she replied wondering why these white folks had dragged her down here to view something she could only dream about. What was it with white folks? Did they have no heart, no compassion? Hadn't she just broken down last night after twenty one years and told them how she had gone unnoticed and was invisible to them only to flaunt the gap between their lifestyle and hers. She was just so tired of their unfeeling, uncaring attitudes. If she hadn't needed this last paycheck she would have left right now.

"Do you like the way it's decorated? I actually did it myself. I thought it would give it a taste of home instead of letting the interior decorators do it. Theirs always seems so cold. This has a homier feel to it. Don't you think?"

"I do," Mattie responded smiling amiably. *'What did he want me to say? And why the hell is he so excited over something I will never ever be able to afford. I hope this isn't one of his schemes to ask me to marry him again. I don't care how much money he has. Our world's are just too far apart.*

51

J.J. was overjoyed.

'And well he should be.' Mattie thought. The place with all of its fixings and trimmings was right out of Better Homes and Gardens with its ten foot ceilings and skylight and the open floor plan was to die for. She especially liked the kitchen with its stainless steel appliances and pots and pans' hanging down over the island. It was out of this world.

The library intrigued her as well. An avid reader the shelves held a variety of books covering a plethora of topics. There was even a small section of African American literature lending her to believe that the prospective tenants would be Black folks. White folks sure were devious. Some small reference would show just how liberal they were and might just be the thing to sway them. Of course the way J.J. was going on about the place it was obvious this was to be his. He'd decorated the loft to his liking an obvious reward for closing the deal yesterday, his first major coup. It was about time he moved away. He probably had more sense than all the rest of the family combined.

"So, you really like it, Mattie?"

"Yes, J.J. I love it. I'm happy for you. I really am. It's about time you cut the apron strings."

Henry Hansborough who had been sitting on the settee nearby on a conference call placed the tiny cell on the table and approached the two who were chattering away.

"Well, Mattie what do you think?"

"Think of what, Mr. Hansborough?"

"The place."

"It's to die for. I was just telling J.J. that it's high time he cut the apron strings and got out on his own."

"I couldn't agree more," he said shooting a part glance at his son. "But we're not here to talk about J.J. We're here to talk about you."

"I'm sorry I don't understand, Mr. Hansborough."

Digging into his wallet he handed Mattie a small piece of paper. Opening it slowly Mattie was speechless.

"A little something in the way of backpay or if you're still inclined to leave us I guess you can call it severance pay. The loft is also yours upon the contingency that you remain in our employ."

Mattie couldn't believe it. Looking at the check with all those zeroes at the end she was at a loss for words.

White folks sure were truly something.

53

Olivia

Lost and Turned Out

At thirty five she had all but thrown the towel in as far as men were concerned. She'd been married once if that's what you wanted to call that fiasco. If she had had half the sense she had now she wouldn't have given him a second thought but she was young and dumb and hungry for a man and before she could get a handle on things she was pregnant. She'd never wanted kids but when she'd gotten pregnant she had little or no choice and both she and Troy had been elated. At the time she really and truly believed that the baby would change him but it wasn't but a month or so after Troy Jr. was born that he was back in the streets again. For the life of her she couldn't figure out what those streets provided that she couldn't provide him. Men adored her-- well that was--every man but Troy who treated her like yesterdays old newspaper.

At first she blamed herself. Yeah, maybe she had picked up a pound or two since the baby but when she wasn't working she was in the gym and looked as good if not better than some of those young girls half her age. And still she could not keep a man. Not long after Troy Jr. was born she caught Troy at Infinity draped over some heifer. And it was right then and there that she decided that he would be the last man that would take advantage of her.

Mommy had all but adopted little Troy and she decided to forget men altogether and just concentrate on doing her. Her father suggested she return to school to get her masters and she welcomed that. At least keeping busy with school and work she wouldn't have too much time to think about Troy and the way that had turned out. She still found time to follow him on facebook and his leaving didn't mean the pain went with him. She cried many a night thinking of what a fool she'd been. She'd given her all and yet when it came to men the results were always the same.

Lil Troy was eleven now and though she felt guilty about not spending as much time as a mother should she knew the boy was her parents saving grace. They simply adored him and she wondered if either of them would still be alive if their grandson wasn't a part of their lives. After awhile the guilt subsided some and when her parents insisted that she focus on her life and career and leave Troy where he had two parents that cared about him, loved him and had nothing but time to dote on him she agreed with some hesitation.

Two years later she graduated Magna Cum Laude from the University of Maryland with a master's degree in Business Marketing and soon afterwards left the firm of James and Peterson to go to work for the feds. The growth potential was greater and the perks. Oh my God the perks!! The federal government had access to the world and with the global economy booming she had a chance to travel as she never had before. So, when the opportunity became available she was on it.

Now for the first time since she couldn't remember when, she was working and being compensated for it. Overall life was good. She had a cute little place in Virginia though she hated the hour long commute in to D.C. everyday. She loved her job and over the past twelve years her meteoric rise within the Department of Agriculture had heads turning. She was now commanding well over six figures. It all seemed to be more than any woman could ask for but there was still one thing missing. A man.

The phone rang jarring Olivia from her thoughts. Placing the wine glass down on the coffee table Olivia picked up the phone only to see Kim's face on her phone. She started not to answer but she'd blown her off for the last two days and knew that if she didn't answer soon her girlfriend would go into panic mode and either have the sheriff's deputies shining flashlights through her windows or she'd show up cussing and fussing talking about how'd she'd been so worried.

"Yes love."

"Damn 'Livia I've been trying to get in touch with you for two days now. You back to not taking calls or is it just me you choose not to talk to?"

"It's just you."

"I'll pretend I didn't hear that. I called you I don't know how many times yesterday."

"I know. I was in meetings most of the day. What was the emergency anyway?"

"It wasn't anything serious. Was just feelin' a lil needy and wanted to see if my bff wanted to come out and play."

"It's been hectic right through here Kimmy. Ever since I got the promotion I haven't had a chance to breathe. And you know we just kicked off this project in South Africa. I have less than three months to assemble a top flight team to put this thing together."

"I hear you. It sounds like you're doing big things but let me ask you something seriously."

"I'm listening."

"Do you live to work or work to live?"

Olivia had to smile. Kimmy had never fashioned to work. As long as her bills were paid she was content to live paycheck to paycheck as long as she had enough money to hit the clubs on weekends and inevitably find a husband to take the drudgery of work from her life.

"Unlike you I love my job," Olivia replied.

"That's beautiful but you know what they say. All work and no play..." Olivia cut her off before she could finish.

"That's what you say. I do all the socializing I need to do at work and am tired of going out to these little dives where men don't want to do anything but make wagers on how long it will take to get in your pants. Half of can't write their names and if you meet one that can chances are he's married, creeping and looking for a night affair."

"Ah, come on 'Livia let's be fair. You and I both know there are a lot of bright, beautiful young brothers out there doing big things. And just because you only attract the bottom feeders doesn't mean you can condemn them all."

Olivia knew Kim was right and for the sake of argument agreed. Now she wished she hadn't answered her best friend's call at all.

"How many times have we had this conversation Kimmy? I hear what you're sayin' and I respect your opinion but that's just not where my head is at now."

"Damn 'Liv a few bad experiences and you're ready to throw the towel in."

"Who said I was throwing anything in? That's just not my focus right now. I'm trying to do me. If I position myself right who knows what may happen. If I'm in the right circles and the right brother comes along then hey! But I'm not going to a sanitation worker's convention to look for a nuclear physicist. If I meet someone in the workplace chances are we're on the same level and share some of the same interests that's a lot better chance of me meeting someone than in those meat markets you go to we're all they do is look at you and wanna know what they're chances are that they'll bed you down before the nights over. I ain't got time for that. I made that mistake more than once and I just ain't gonna keep setting myself up to get my feelings hurt and my ass beat."

"I hear ya but you know my philosophy. You gotta be in it to win it. You can't be standing on the sidelines and think you gonna take home the game ball."

"I don't know what you don't get. I ain't playing no games."

"Okay. Okay. Chill woman. You wanna stay home and turn into an old hag then so be it but let me tell you who I saw last night looking just as fine as he wanted to. I mean this fool looked good enough for me to drop to my knees in the middle of the club."

"Oh hell, that could have been any ol' body for you slut," Olivia laughed.

"I'm just gonna ignore that but seriously guess who I bumped to at the club last night?"

"Go ahead. Tell me before you bust wide open and have a seizure," Olivia laughed.

"Remember that guy who used to chase you around and was calling you relentlessly. What was his name?"

"Andre," Olivia whispered.

"Yeah. That's him. And damn wash he looking good last night. Say, whatever happened to him? You used to talk about him all the time. I was almost sure he was gonna be the one who was gonna scrape the cobwebs off your coochie."

"I gotta go," Olivia replied before swiping her hand against the power button ending the call.

Forgetting all etiquette Olivia grabbed the wine bottle and drank freely from the bottle. Andre or Dre was the last guy she had been involved with and was the straw that broke the camel's back.

Like all of them it had seemed harmless enough. She'd met him on a night out with Kim at Tacoma Station. All in all, it had seemed innocent enough and every time she looked up she caught him staring at her through those big, brown marble eyes and she had to admit he was one fine specimen of a man. Standing nearly six foot two he was neatly attired in a charcoal gray suit, white shirt and gray and black striped tie. His shoes alone cost more than her whole outfit including the matching Michael Kors bag and shoes she was so fond of. Delicious, Olivia thought taking him all in. Moments later he was buying a round of drinks for both she and Kim but there was little doubt that his eyes were fixed on her and her alone. And after several dances she found herself totally taken in by his smooth talk and laid back charm. Hours later she'd rather hesitantly and after much prompting from Kim she'd given in and given him her number never expecting him to actually follow up. But call he did and before long she looked forward to his calls. He called every day at seven and after awhile Olivia found herself rushing home as to not miss his nightly call.

Over time she learned that he was an investment banker for Merill Lynch and a fitness trainer but in the month that followed their initial meeting not once had he mentioned sex or following up on their meeting. Rather he seemed content to just call and listen to her go on and on about her day. She liked that. But in time Olivia began to wonder why he didn't at least ask her out on a date. Nowadays there were so many reasons. He could be married or sexually challenged. You just didn't know but it did seem strange here in D.C. where men would grope and feel and do everything short of try to sex you right there in the club.

But not Dre. No Dre was cool and she figured that as good as he looked and with his job and portfolio he could probably have his pick of the litter so she was sure that's why he was as cautious as any woman. Olivia was cool with the feeling out period but after a month and a half she wasn't even sure what he looked like. One thing she did know was that he like very few outside of Troy stirred something deep inside of her. How many times had she had to cut the conversation short just so she wouldn't say something that would let him know that she was his for the taking then find herself lying in bed wondering, wanting him to take her in his arms.

After a month or so they agreed to meet downtown in Union Station for lunch. Nothing fancy, just a chance to get together. And Lord knows he looked even better than he had the first time she'd seen him but by this time it wasn't his looks that had her. It was his soft-spoken charm and his attentiveness to her every need that endeared him to her so. By the time they parted company she knew little more about him than she did before but if there was one thing she did know and that was that she was going to have him before the week was out.

She must have had a glow about her because more than one of her secretaries commented about her radiance. Even those in her secretarial pool that looked at her with cold steely eyes usually spoke today. And the day seemed to drag on forever. She couldn't wait till he called her tonight but she couldn't wait for that and no sooner had she exited the federal building than she called Kim.

"What's up Kimmy?"

"You tell me lady. You sound like you just hit pay dirt. You number come up?"

"Better than that. I had lunch with Dre."

"Finally. Damn. Where did he take you?"

"Oh, no it wasn't like that. He was taking the train in from Philly so I just met him in Union Station and we grabbed a bite. Kimmy let me tell you. The man is fine. I think I got wet just sitting across from him."

"What are you wearing?"

"Nothing special. I'm rocking this little lavender Jones of New York skirt suit and some black pumps. I had meetings all day so I had to look somewhat conservative you know. Couldn't really rock his world the way I wanted to."

"Okay so what happened? Give me the skinny."

"Nothing really. We just talked--you know--small talk. I figure if he wants to play it coy and close to the vest I can do that too."

"Whoa! Whoa! 'Livia! Here's the thing. Some people can play hard to get. You ain't one of them. When's the last time you even had a date before Dre came a calling? I know it's been over a year."

"What exactly are you trying to imply Kimmy?"

"No, no, no. Don't get me wrong Liv. You are one beautiful sister. Most of these chicks in D.C. would hand over their first born to have your looks. On top of that you're sharp as whip but when it comes to men you're like the Orkin man. You can rid yourself of a man the way he rids a ghetto tenement of roaches."

"Very funny heifer. I see you got jokes today."

"I wish I did. All ahm saying is that after a year long slump I don't think that playing hard to get is not the right tactic for you. How's that been working for you so far?"

"Go to hell Kimmy!"

"All I'm saying is those playing hard to get more often than not don't get got. And especially in D.C. Do you know the ratio of beautiful women to straight, eligible brothers with something going on? It's gotta be something like 20-1."

"I hear you baby girl. That's why I invited him over Saturday night."

"No you didn't! Oooh girl, you must really be feelin' ol' boy. I think the last time you invited a guy over was little Petey Hamill. You remember little Petey Hamill with the runny nose and the cleft lip."

"You're crazy," Olivia laughed.

"I'm serious. You were crazy about him and invited him to your first birthday party in second grade," Kim laughed.

"Oh shut the hell up," Olivia said still laughing as she made her way through the turnstiles at the Metro. "I don't even know why I let you into my world."

"Cause you love me baby and I'm the only one that tells you the truth."

"Listen I gotta go Kimmy. My train's here. I'll call you and let you know how it all turns out."

"You better."

It was Saturday morning her morning to sleep in but not only was she engulfed in the sunlight flooding her bedroom but also with the idea of the day that loomed before her. She had so much to do and so little time. Up until now she'd been selective, picky even weighing the few men she talked to. But Dre was a no brainer and although she wasn't particularly fond of having to pursue a man if there was one man that deserved her pursuits it was Dre. She smiled at the mere thought of him before hitting the floor on the run and heading for the shower. There was so much to do. Showering quickly Olivia threw on her favorite Carolina blue sweat suit grabbed her purse and her car keys and headed for the silver Audi parked across the street from her townhouse. Turning the key the smooth sounds of Kem flooded the car. Easing the car into drive she headed for the beltway when the phone rang.

"Auntie Liv are you still coming?"

Damn. So preoccupied with her own thoughts she had completely forgotten Shana. This was her weekend to pick up Shana. For the past three or four years she'd picked up the nine year old and spent the day with her doing anything the child had a mind to do. It had started as a favor to Kim who was in the midst of an ugly break up from an abusive husband. She'd gone to pick Kim up one Saturday evening when then husband Shane and Kim were in the midst of a heated argument. The little girl stood and watched helplessly while her parents went back and forth. Not thinking it a particularly healthy atmosphere for a five year old Olivia grabbed a few of Shana's belongings and whisked her out of the house until things calmed down. Four months later things had still not calmed down and Shana became a fixture in Olivia's household. Kim's eventual divorce brought Shana back home but not without trepidation from Olivia who still did not view Kim's lifestyle as appropriate for raising a child. So, in an attempt to show her an alternative to Kim's lifestyle. And of course in the interim she had fallen in love with Shana and basically adopted her as her own. Getting off at the next exit Olivia backtracked and sped towards Kim's house when the phone rang again.

"Hey girl," came Kim's voice sounding huskier than usual.

"Rough night huh?"

"I think I had a few too many Supermans."

"The drink or the men."

"Both honey," Kim laughed. "Went to the Half Note in Maryland with Michelle and it was packed like I've never seen it. Faces was playing... you know the all girls band. And I mean they was rockin' the joint. I ain't seen that many good lookin' brothers in one place in a long time. Every time I looked up here comes another one tryin' to buy me a drink and I was cordial so I accepted. Girl! Let me tell you I could barely walk when it was time to go. I don't know what she was doing but around two I bumped into her and she come talking about leaving and going to Charades. I was like the only place I'm going is home and get in my bed."

"And how's that working for you today?"

"It's not. I got a hangover like you wouldn't believe. Feel like Ray Rice punched the hell out of me," she laughed.

"Not funny Kim."

"I know and when Shana came waking me this morning I wanted to tell her where she could go but all she wanted to know was where her sneakers were so she could be ready when you came to pick her up. I was like thank God for 'Livia. She told me she'd already called you and I didn't think anything of it until now."

"Why what's up?"

"Aren't you entertaining tonight?"

"Yeah. And?"

"Well, with you having your first date in over a year I'm thinking that you gonna need all the time you need. You got to get your nails done and your hair did and get the coochie waxed. I know it's like a jungle down there," she said laughing hysterically. "Man gonna think he's on a safari when he hits that bush," Kim said laughing so hard tears ran down her face. "Hold on someone's at the door. Probably them damn Jehovah Witnesses."

Putting the phone down and opening the door Kim stood there in shock.

"No, it ain't the Jehovah Witnesses but Lord knows you need God up in here."

"Auntie Liv," Shana cried running and jumping in Olivia's arms.

"Damn. I don't get that kind of reception and I put food on the table for the little heifer."

"Ahh mommy," Shana whined.

"You ready to go sweetheart? Can't get you out of this den of sin quick enough."

"Yes, I'm ready Aunt Liv. I just have to run upstairs and get my toothbrush."

"No, Shana. You don't need your toothbrush this time. You're not spending the night tonight. Maybe next weekend."

"But why mommy?"

"Because auntie has something important to do this weekend. Now run upstairs and grab your jacket."

The girl dropped her head in obvious disappointment.

"You start that pouting and you won't be going anywhere young lady. I'll keep you right here with me."

"Oh, hell a fate worse than death," Olivia laughed.

"That's what I was calling you for. I was trying to tell you that you didn't have to come pick Shana up. I could have told her you were busy."

"And miss my girl? She's the best female company I have," Olivia said staring straight at Kim and smiling.

"But seriously Liv, you need a night like this where you can let your hair down and just enjoy yourself."

"I can't agree with you more but not at the expense of hurting my little girl," she said grabbing Shana's hand and skipping towards the door. "We should be back no later than six or seven."

What time's your appointment?"

"When I finish with my little girl," Olivia replied.

By six that evening Olivia was worn out. They'd been to Tyson's Corner shopping and then over to the National Harbor just because it was one of the girl's favorite places in the whole wide world according to her.

Running late Olivia didn't have a clue as to where she was going to summon the energy to entertain tonight but when she called to cancel she was surprised to hear that he was five minutes from her place.

Olivia remembered telling him the key was in the mailbox as if it were yesterday. She still had to drop Shana off and with no time to cook she'd stop by Three Brothers and pick up a couple of veal ptarmiagiana dinners and then grab a bottle of wine on the way in. At the most it would take no more than forty five minutes to an hour.

Arriving home little more than an hour later Olivia was surprised to find Dre, remote in hand reclining in the easy chair fast asleep. She smiled and dreamed of the day Dre in the easy chair would become a permanent fixture. For now she would be content to just let him sleep while she showered and prepared dinner.

Hours later Olivia closed her eyes. Dinner was great, the conversation better and the gentleness in which he took her convinced her that this was the only man for her. After months of little more than getting to know one another there was little doubt in her mind that this was truly her soul mate. She felt his firm body against hers as she closed her eyes and drifted off to sleep her mind fixated on having this man, possessing him. The only thing that bothered her about Dre and their budding relationship was that at no time in the six months since she'd known him had he even come close to committing himself to her. They'd, well at least she had, brought up how she felt about commitment and marriage. And though he'd listened he never once uttered a word explaining how he felt. And as she closed her eyes she knew that if she were ever convinced that she wanted to be in a wholly monogamous and committed relationship with anyone it was this man.

The following morning Olivia woke to the sound of birds chirping outside her window and sunlight bathing her. The night had been glorious. She couldn't remember how many times they'd made love but it hadn't been enough. It was glorious and all she could think of was recreating the joy she felt and was mildly surprised to turn and find a note where Dre had been.

'Went out for my morning run. Will scrounge up breakfast on my way back.'

She smiled as she tried to gather her thoughts and pull herself together. The phone rang.

"Hey girl. Is he still there?"

"No. Actually he went out to grab breakfast."

"Breakfast? So, you didn't scare him away. So, how was he? Was he as good as he looks?"

72

"Better," Olivia said grinning widely now. "Boy had me in tears."

"Damn. You sound like you're all in. He must be something if that old cob webbed, black widow pussy didn't scare him away. My girl is all in!"

"What's that mean?"

"That means you're half a heartbeat from the "L" word."

"I could very well be. If I were he would certainly be the one. But let me get off this phone. He should be on his way back and I look like I've been through the war. Tell Shana I'll be there no later than twelve."

"The hell with Shana. You stay with that man. Hell, I can't even remember the last time you had a man spend time let alone stay the night."

Olivia laughed.

"Go to hell, Kim."

"I'm just teasin'. So what do you have planned for the day?"

"I'm not sure. I'm leavin' all that up to him. But if I had my preferences I'd stay in bed all day and let him revisit that old—what did you call it—that black widow pussy just as many times as he wanted to. I forgot just how good some good dick feels when applied properly," Olivia laughed.

"I feel you."

"Let me go Kim. I think that's him at the door."

"You go girl. Call me when he leaves and give me the skinny."

"Talk to you later."

The afternoon proceeded just as Olivia had hoped until somewhere around round five when she passed out. It wasn't until the next morning when she awoke again. Olivia grinned. Dre was gone and in a way she was glad. Another tryst like that and she'd be forced to call EMS. Picking up her phone there were no texts. Looking at the clock she noticed it was ten after eight. She was running late again. Jumping up she ran to the bath and turned on the shower.

The warm water felt good as it cascaded over her body soothing the pain between her legs. She only wished she could have stayed longer but a quick shower was all she could manage. She was already late. Dressing quickly she grabbed her pocket and searched for her keys. Unable to find them she was glad she had an extra set. When it rained it poured. Grabbing the coffee pot she poured her morning cup and poured two Splendas and a dash of the French vanilla creamer she'd become so fond of and went to reach for a spoon only to find her silverware gone. Thinking nothing of it she went to the dishwasher only to find it empty too. Though puzzled all she could think of was the corporate meeting scheduled to start in fifteen minutes. Grabbing her keys Olivia rushed out the front door of the townhouse only to find her car gone as well.

Blessing or Curse

Y'all probably recollect me telling you about Beulah and Mamie. I always say they my two best friends. I love 'em both to death. I guess they more like sistas to me. We spend alla our time together when we ain't doin' massa's biddin'. And it ain't that we do all that much. I mean what is they're to do other than fish and cook and eat. But we do is enjoy each other's company. None of us is much into men as men folk can cause a gal a whole lot more trouble than they worth. White and niggra.

Why just last week massa found out one of his house niggras—a pretty lil gal—by the name of Sallie Mae who massa had been eyeing for some time come up pregnant by some ol' boy from ova the next plantation. When massa heard he took exception sayin' that he owned her and she shouldn't be pregnant by no no-account field nigga. That's what he said. Then he demanded to know who the boy was. When Sallie Mae refused to tell who the boy was he beat her then raped her and let her know that he was going to sell the baby just as soon as it was born. And Lord knows what he woulda done if he find out who the niggra was that knocked her up. Now we gots to keep a close eye on her so as she don't go and do nothin' foolish.

But that's just why it's best to keep to oneself and to stay away from men folk at any cost. They trouble. I don't meant that niggra mens is bad or nothin'. It's just that when massa own you he think he supposed to be the only man in your life since he owns you.

This here slavery can be a tricky thing though. You can swear off of all those thangs that are bound to provoke massa and still wind up in a whole heap of trouble just because. Like I said this tang called slavery is one winding river with its share of dangerous currents, rapids and undertows which brings me back to my good friend Beulah.

I can't recollect if I told you about Beulah but she's one of the most beautiful womans I know. She easily the purtiest on this here plantation wit' ova three hundred slaves. She like a lot of us ain't rightly sho' who her mammy or pappy was but from the looks of her she a cross between a African and some white man and the reason I say that is because she got the prettiest brown complexion. It's almost like she been bronzed and though she stands about six feet tall and considered a big woman she got really thin features. She sho nuff mixed with something. But she ain't highfalutin or stuck up because of her looks. No. Beulah is just as humble and down to earth a person as you want to find. And that's one of the reasons I love her so.

Everyday someone—men and women—alike are coming up sayin' somethin' regarding her looks. Even the children walk up and stare at her and say things like, 'Miss is yours eyes brown. I ain't neva seen no niggra wit' light brown eyes befo'. They sho is purty.' And Beulah would just smile and say thank you and keep it movin'.

The men folk were absolutely crazy about her but no matter what they'd say she always seem a little embarrassed by all the attention and would change the subject by asking if we thought she was getting too fat.

"Too fat? Girl if you was any thinner we'd have to send out a search party just to find you."

We'd laugh but we knew Beulah was uncomfortable every time someone would comment on her looks.

One day I asked her straight out. I sayed to her.

"Beulah why you hate it so when people say you a pretty woman?"

Now you gotta know Beulah. And if you do you know Beulah took her time about just about everything and it was no different when it came time to answer a simple question but then there was nothing simple about my friend and I could feel the hairs growing on my head as I waited for her to answer my question.

"Let me ask you a question June."

"I'm listening."

"What would you say if someone said you one of Massa John's field niggras?"

"Don't suppose I'd say anything."

"And why not?"

"Cause that's pretty clear to see."

"Exactly. And the truth about it is you ain't had nothin' to do with your lot in life. So, when people say I's purty or you got light eyes what am I suppose to say? I ain't had nothin' to do wi' that. Now if they say Beulah you is one sweet person well then I know I had somethin' to do with that. I work at tryna be a sweet person. You unnerstand?"

"I guess I do."

"What's important to me is what I make of m'self not what God give me. He blessed me with these looks I guess but he ain't tellin' me that that's all I got to do is be good lookin'."

That blessing soon became a curse as white folk and niggras alike commented on her spectacular beauty. Soon massa got wind of this when several of his guests commented asking about her and if he was interested in parceling out her services. When missy got wind of this she was vehemently opposed and thought it would serve them better with the end of the slave trade right around the corner if they simply matched her with the biggest, strongest, most handsome bucks on the place and let her breed.

Oh, how much they could make from the sale of her offspring. And so missy decided that it would be her own special project to start breeding Beulah which all came as a shock to Beulah.

I remember the day as if it were yesterday.

"I just left the big house. Seems Missy wants to have a word with you," Mamie said addressing Beulah as we sat there talking and shucking a bushel of field peas.

"You sho you got the right person. You know yo' blind ass cain't see," Beulah laughed.

"Might cain't see but yo' big ass is kinda hard to miss," Mamie shot back.

"Am I gittin' big?" Beulah said turning to me.

"As hell," I said laughing at her as she rose and rose and rose. "I swear you gittin' taller by the minute," I said looking at Mamie and laughing.

"You better git on up there. You know how she is. You don't git up there in her time her butt will be down here stirrin' up trouble for everybody."

"Yeah. But whatever it is you know it cain't be good. She ain't nothin' but the anti-Christ. The damn devil reincarnate."

"Well, go on and git it over wit'. We'll be here to wipe your tears when you get back," I said.

No call up to the big house ever came to any good. We all knew that especially after quitting time in the fields. It just meant white folks was thinking up some more devilment and as long it didn't pertain to you it was good but when they called Beulah it might as well have been Mamie or me going. Anything that affected one of us affected us all but for the life of me and Mamie we couldn't figure it out. Far as we knew missy just wanted Beulah to make her some new gown for some debutante's ball or something of that nature.

When Beulah came back walking even slower than usual we knew it was more than just some sewing that missy wanted done.

"You look like you just lost yo best friend and as you can plainly see I's right here so what's bothering you?"

Beulah had that faraway look and ignored me completely. Whatever had happened must have been devastating.

"Mamie do you have any more of that homemade hooch you're always trying to get someone to taste."

"Sure got some of ol' man Water's grain alcohol from his still and some of my own elderberry wine I just made. Choose your poison dear but let me tell you that grain will knock you on your... And if you got to get up and head down to the lower forty you may not want to mess with either. Especially you Beulah... You know you ain't no drinker," Mamie said.

"I've got another proposition for you sweetheart. Why don't you just run it by Mamie and me and we'll see if we can't work it out before you commence to get tore up."

"Ain't nthin' you can do 'bout this one. But I need a drink before I even think about telling you what this old crazy heifer has in store for me now."

"That bad?" I asked.

"Yeah. It's that bad June. Mamie bring some of that grain."

Mamie went running off to her cabin and I sat there dumbfounded. Beulah was always the one that could make the darkest moments seem bright and I had never seen her like this. Always one to find a silver lining in a patch work quilt I knew this had to be bad.

"Here you go darling now tell mammy Mamie what's troubling you?"

Beulah gulped the half of glass of grain alcohol and gasped for air.

"You ready now? Whatever it is it can't be that bad and even if it is we've never let a bukhra get the best of us."

"Mamie have you been sipping too? What the hell is wrong with you? You see she's got somethin' on her mind. Would you please give her a chance to talk."

Beulah looked up.

"You two stop it. I have to leave. That's all there is to it. President Lincoln can't declare war soon enough. But I have some money saved up and I will pay someone, anyone for a chance to help me escape. I know this is going to put you in harm's way but I need you to help me escape."

"Running away has always appealed to me sista but why the necessity now. Please tell us why the urgency?"

"I'll tell you why June. Missy called me up to the big house to inform me that she and Massa John could utilize me best by taking me out of the fields and making me a breeder," Beulah said dropping her head. I watched. Her shoulders heaved but there was no sound as the tears dropped like April rain.

"She wants you to be a breeder?" Mamie said with some surprise. "Does she know that you are a good Christian woman and not the least bit interested in fornication? Perhaps she meant to call me." Mamie laughed.

"Oh hush Mamie. And how do she propose to do this?" I asked somewhat naively.

"They are to build me a shack closer to the ridge and missy is to ovasee it. She is to choose the men that frequent it and they are to bed me down until I become with child and she will appoint someone to stay with me and look after me until the child is born at which time they will auction off the child to the highest bidder and then I will start again."

"And no more of the fields from can't see in the morning 'til can't see at night. Is that what I'm to understand you're telling me?" Mamie said in attempt to lift her spirits. "Ask her if she needs another breeder." Mamie chuckled as she poured herself another cupful.

"Pour me some too," I said in disbelief. "After this I believe I need some too."

"White folks is truly something." I muttered taking the cup. "She don't even know you."

"Iffen she did she'd know Beulah was the last person to ask. Not to get too personal but has you ever been with a man?"

"No. And I ain't got no notion to 'til I'm legal and married."

"And tomorrow you's to be a breeder."

Mamie laughed aloud.

"I believe this calls for a round all around," Mamie said pouring a tad in each cup.

"She say she gonn give me a week for me to get my head fixed in the right way. Then she gonna set me up with Shekura."

"Whew! That ain't somebody you break a girl in with her first time. He liable to maim you for life," Mamie laughed.

"Okay. On your way. It's time for you to head home with your drunk ass."

"Ahh stop June. Beulah knows I'm just tryna make light of a bad situation."

"This is too serious to joke about Mamie."

"I'm just gonna run June. They say President Lincoln's on the verge of calling for war any day and maybe just maybe if he does I can get caught up in all the confusion and make my way north."

"It would have to be a whole heap of confusion and chaos for your pretty ass to go unnoticed," Mamie said and despite her drunken state I knew she was right.

"No, baby you can't run. We gots ta just figger something else out. But don't worry me and Mamie will figger something out. We ain't never let you down before has we?"

I couldn't sleep that night with Beulah on my mind. It was a difficult situation and I didn't see many viable options but it wasn't Beulah that kept me up. What kept me up was that these very same white folks that ran around preachin' and praisin' the Lord couldn't see that slavery was no more than a den of inequity—a den of sin—and niggras was no more than farm animals but not even the farm animals were used and abused like us niggras. I was angry. I had been angry for years and it had always been Beulah who had warned me about becoming so bitter that it would somehow change my own spirit. She used to say to me. 'June don't let their wickedness make you sinful and evil as well. You remain pure and put their inequities in the hands of the good Lord. He will part the

Red Sea like he did for the Israelites and lead us out of bondage. You just have to faith and patience.'

I listened to this woman with her beautiful soul and now this. I didn't curse Jesus but I certainly wanted to know how her faith and patience were serving her now. They say Jesus helps those that help themselves and I knew that this good Christian would soon be a whore through no fault of her own and decided that in the end death was still death whether it be a quick end or endured slowly. And by the end of the night I'd come up with one conclusion and that was that today we would begin our escape.

"You're certainly cheerful this morning," I said rather sarcastically to Mamie.

"Head is on fire," she muttered.

"And it ain't nothin' like it's gonna be 'rond midday when that sun is right overhead."

"Thanks June. Just what I needed to hear... Did you give any thought to Beulah's situation?"

"Yeah was up all night thinking about it. I gotta feeling I'm not going to be the only one suffering come midday. So what did you come up with?"

"We run."

"That's your plan? I don't know if you're aware of the punishment for runaway slaves and why am I running anyway?

Missy ain't hardly interested in taking me outta these fields and having me pleasured all day and all night and if she was the only place I'd be running would be to bed," Mamie laughed. "Seriously though I did give it some thought and she'd have a good chance going south into Florida and joining Osceola and the black Seminoles. It's a much shorter journey than trying to make it North. She can stay there until Lincoln declares war on the South. Then she can go North. What do you think?"

"I didn't get that far. I just know she's got no choice but to run. But that makes sense. Now c'mon we've got to hurry. Missy said she's going to give her some time to think about it but who knows how much time that is. Could be today... Could be tomorrow... Just can't tell with that crazy white woman."

"So what are you saying?"

"I say we get this day outta the way. Go back to the quarters and have Beulah pack us up while we get some sleep and leave at dark."

"Think she'll go for it?"

"I think she was ready when missy gave her the news. I don't think we'll get any argument there."

"I'll get word to her so she don't spend her day worryin'."

Tempers were short that evening. I guess it was the peril of our upcoming journey into the unknown. None of us had been off the place for more than a day or two. In my case, the only time I'd been away from this here plantation was when they brought me here and that was six or seven years ago. I ain't know no more about Georgia or Florida than a man on the moon. All I knew is that's where runaways escape to and would be protected by black Seminoles who were escaped slaves at one time or another and who had set up villages and colonies with the protection of the Indians and the Spanish. And right now that was as good a place as any and it was close.

None of us were in a p'ticularly good move but found ol' man Lucious who was close to ninety and who coupled as a blacksmith when he wasn't runnin' errands here and there for massa. We knew we could count on Lucius who had spent much of his younger life trying to escape. In fact Lucius tried escaping so many times that a previous matter had chopped off half of his leg to try and stop him from running. But Lucius still ran.

The story goes that he spent eight years with the Seminoles until the longing for his wife and kids led him back here where he's spent the last twenty years. His wife had long since passed on and his kids had either grown and started families of their own or been sold off but we knew that if there was anyone that knew the lay of the land it was Lucius.

"I haven't seen my good friend John Horse in a good many years. You know he and I founded the niggra town of Freetown. All niggra town and we prospered too. We wasn't just no ragtag bunch of runaways. We worked hard and built that community. We traded with the Spanish and they came to respect us as did the Seminoles and the British. We even did some trading with some good white folks along the Florida Georgia border. I'm sho John will welcome three beautiful young ladies into Freetown if I know John," he chuckled.

"Can you show us how to get there?"

"You're asking a lot from an old man. It's been many a year since I made that journey successfully but you must know I tried on at least half a dozen trips. And let me tell you they won't go easy on you when they catch you."

"If they catch us," Mamie said.

The old man smiled.

"Oh they'll catch you. Especially you three who don't know east from west and probably ain't never been offa this here place. I lost my leg trying to make that trip."

"If you help us we can make it," I said not really believing the words coming from my mouth.

"You seemed pretty determined so I'll tell you as much as I know but let me warn you there are a lot of things that you're gonna run into besides just slave catchers. There are the swamps with snakes and alligators bigger than any you've ever seen or wanna see and there are mosquitoes that carry malaria and everyone Indian you run into ain't friendly and like I said any one of those can be just as bad if not worse than the slave catcher. Now you still determined to go?"

"We ain't got no choice Lucius," I admitted.

"I knew it had to be more than just wanting to get away from here with President Lincoln on the verge of declaring war. What's so pressing that y'all got to go right now?"

"Missy wants to make us breeders," I said so as not to single out Beulah.

The old man hung his head.

"White folks never seem to surprise me," he said seeming to understand our situation better now. "Okay what I'm going to tell you is a lot for one person to unnerstand so what I'm going to do is break it down into three parts and each of you will be responsible for knowing your part. It's at most a two day journey."

When old man Lucius finished I wondered if we were in over our heads but the die was cast and so we took his knowledge and went back to our huts and gathered the few belongings that meant something to us and waited for the sun to go down. Tomorrow was Sunday so we knew we had at least a day's head start on the slave catchers and patrollers. When we had assembled everything we started out and headed for the woods as Lucius had directed. No sooner had we gotten into the woods we heard noises. Had we been set up?

"Hurry up ladies! There is no time to waste," Lucius whispered.

Granny

"You know I am going to be ninety seven on my next birthday. Oh, I've lived a long time alright. Sometime's I think I've lived more than a couple of lifetimes in this one lifetime. You see I was never one to lolly-gag around like a lot of folks do nowadays. They wanna tell you why it's okay to rest up and laze around and stay in bed and I tell them all to go to hell. They ain't gonna convince me of anything of the sort.

I always said I only gots one life to live and I'm gonna run it to the motherfuckin' wheels fall off. Yes siree. That's what ahm aimin' to do. Run it to the motherfuckin' wheels fall off. And let me tell you this. All those that were tryna convince me that I should stay home and lay around and relax is dead and gone and I'm still here. Still kickin' up a little fuss. Yes I am at ninety seven I'm still here. You know people is amazed that I still get around on my own volition. Had a young white boy ast me just the other day. Oh, I'd say he was about fifty, fifty-five. He say 'Miss Margaret if you had to attribute one thing to your longevity what would you say it was?' That's what he ast me. And I shocked him. Yes I did. I likes to shock white folks. Always did. Anyway, I telled him if I had to ascribe one thing to my longevity it's getting some good, long sweet dick once a week. Then I fell out right there in his office. He got to lookin' around for his nurses or somebody, anybody to get him away from this old crazy Black woman but I wouldn't let him go. I grabbed him by his suit jacket and said 'Seriously doctor you have to stay loosened up so I suggest some real good sex at least once a week. It done kept me purring since I was twelve and it don't much matter who your partner is as long as they can hit that sweet spot and make it purr. Then I fell out again. I had to let his ass go 'cause he looked like he was ready to fall out and I won't about to adminster no CPR to some damn cracker."

"Granny you ain't prejudiced is you?"

"Hell no baby girl. I just can't stand white people is all. I deal with 'em. I mean I can interact civilly but I just don't like 'em. I believe that's just something I was born with. It's in my genes. Most colored folks from the South got that gene. It's not something you learn. It's something you're born with. I believe it's in my chromosomes, my DNA like Sickle Cell. It's not a conscious thing. Sometimes I goes to sleep at night and I wake up in cold sweats and I'm so damn angry that I'm having these dreams."

"What's in those dreams grandma?"

"Now I know you supposed to be tracing your family tree but some of what I'm telling you are family secrets like traditions and you can't go letting the world know what all family secrets we gots."

"Okay grandma but you still haven't told me why you woke up in cold sweats."

"Well, yes as I was telling you I'm not and have no desire to hate any man or any race of people 'cause I'm a Christian woman and always have been and always will be but like I said I have this bad gene I inherited and I have this recurring dream of Nat Turner's Slave Insurrection when he went from plantation-to-plantation murdering what they likes to refer to as innocent white folks."

"I don't think you waking up in a cold sweat makes you prejudiced or a bad person grandma. What he did murdering innocent people was a horrible thing."

"Oh, no. Don't get me wrong child that's not why I break out in hives and cold sweats."

"Then why grandma?"

"I breaks out in cold sweats because he didn't finish the job and kill all of them crackers. That's what upsets me so."

A Day in the Life

Ask me how I'm feeling? And I'll tell you I'm feeling like shit. Can't shake it either... I'm frustrated. I'm angry. Want to fuck something up right through here. Want to hurt something... Want to burn this bitch down...

No matter how hard I try I just can't seem to get it done. I was sitting in the doctor's office this morning. I'd called them at around nine a.m. this morning trying to have one of my prescriptions refilled and Robin, the Black receptionists told me they'd call me when the doctor had written the prescription and I could come by and pick it up on my way to the pharmacy.

I waited until three for them to call me and when I had heard nothing I promptly put on my winter coat which did little to prevent the blustery winds and snow as well as my one glove and walked over to the doctor's office to ask about the status of prescription and was told by the old, nasty, white receptionist that it wasn't ready and if they told me they would call why didn't I just stay at home and wait for the call.

Now I've had a few doctors since I was first diagnosed with heart disease, high blood pressure, and diabetes and it has been rather easy to see which doctors have a really good bedside manner, those that were genuinely interested in my health and those that couldn't give a damn.

My last doctor had no bedside manner to speak of but was proficient in his craft and I respected him immensely. But with my changing locations it was close to a two hour commute each way in order to get to him. (Now I wonder if it wasn't worth the inconvenience). And so I changed doctors as a matter of convenience. My current doctor, who will rename nameless, has neither bedside manner nor my health or best interest at heart. If I told him I needed cocaine to help me with my sluggishness he would have simply asked how much and in what form. He clearly was not interested in this little Black man who he saw quarterly.

In any case, I walked to his office being that it was Friday and my health was of little concern to him. He maintained what seemed to me something more akin to banker's hours than a doctor's office hours. In any case, I was told that I could have a seat if I cared to wait until the doctor had a chance to get around to me. And being that my doctor has banker's hours I decided to wait or else I would suffer through the weekend with migraines from lack of medication.. By the time he took the time to scratch off some illegible hieroglyphics I'd read everything from Ebony to Better Homes

100

and Gardens. When I was finally called to get the prescription I was chastised like I was a six year old child instead of a fifty six year old man and former school teacher who had authored thirteen novels.

"Mr. Brown the doctor said he will not issue another prescription until you come in for another visit," the receptionist said disgustedly.

I bit down hard. A Black man in the land of the free and home of the brave must learn to bite down hard if he would like to live a full yet encumbered life. What I wanted to say is, 'who the hell are you speaking to in that tone bitch?' Instead I said quite politely I might add that the doctor's office usually notifies or sends me some type of correspondence making me aware that my quarterly visit is due. She ignored my comments surprised that I had not only had the nerve to answer a white woman back but probably equally as surprised that I could speak aside from groans and some other guttural nuances that resembled language.

She promptly scheduled me for the following week. It had been three months, one quarter exactly since I had last seen him but I know that if I had not stopped by they wouldn't have informed me of that or anything else. I was not a priority but simply just a consumer a cash cow with an insurance card.

Walking home in the bitter Pittsburgh cold I thought about when I was a child and my doctor would stop by the house when I was sick. Those days were long gone and I wondered how long it would be before we had drive through physicals. I pulled the hood around my head to ward off the biting wind and picked up my pace. Two blocks from home two SUV's and two police cars pulled up alongside of me. I stopped immediately, well schooled in the art of subjugating myself to the powers that be.

"What's your name?

"Hezekiah Brown," I answered. I wanted to ask why but knowing my place I thought better of it.

"Okay. You're not the person we're looking for. Person we're looking for has on a blue hoodie."

Well, the hoodie I had on was blue and white striped and so if that was the general description I guess I fit it. The unsaid description I'm sure went something like this. Black male wearing a blue hoodie... I'm sure it went on to mention approximate height and weight but the key words in the description were Black male. It could have been any Black male. After all we were all criminals. It was in our genes. That's how we were seen but and as much as I wanted to scream and shout and tear into them for having stopped me against my will I knew better. And though I had no civil rights under the conditions I was relieved. I was relieved that I had not been utterly humiliated and been frisked, thrown into the back of one of the four police vehicles and detained until they had run my record and were sure that I had not perpetrated any crime. I was relieved that I could walk away. In my fifty six years I have come to like breathing. In any case, I wasn't frisked, detained or arrested.

This could have easily taken place as it had on numerous occasions but I was adept at knowing my role as a nigga in a world I had no place being, didn't belong and was not welcomed or accepted.

I was not protesting, demonstrating or committing any crime but was simply rushing trying to get out of the cold. However, the fact that I was walking in sub-zero temperatures was an in indication that I was too poor to own a vehicle and therefore was at the mercy of white America. The fact that I was a college graduate, came from a well-to-do home, had travelled somewhat extensively never came into play. After all there was one common denominator, one prevailing factor that negated all the aforementioned. I was Black and therefore reduced to suffering all the indignities of a Jew in Nazi Germany who did not have the necessary credentials sewn to my lapel. But then I did not need the Star of David pinned to my lapel. My very hue was my defining mark.

At home I seethed. Torn between emotions I hated the fact that I had been stopped for wearing clothing to protect me from the elements. I was angry that my skin color was in and of itself an indictment which rendered me vulnerable to such actions by this Gestapo we call law enforcement. And to my surprise I vowed never to wear that hoodie again as if that was going to save my Black ass. And then I thought of the movie I'd just seen called Selma depicting the life of Martin Luther King Jr. Not once did I see the good reverend in anything other than a suit and tie and how many times had he been jailed not for the way he was dressed but for the color of his skin.

I was angry and knew from my reading that as Frederick Douglass said the only way to overcome slavery, racism, and to affect change is to 'agitate, agitate, agitate'.

This I believe as I strongly believe it is equally as important to educate, educate, educate. And in so doing we can afford young Black boys like I was the only arsenal available to those of us of limited means to combat this brutally racist society without unwittingly becoming victims of it.

I gave up teaching some years ago as well as actively fighting against racism. Oh, I still hold firm to my beliefs but simply have traded in my picket sign for a pen and paper. Frederick Douglass' words are still firmly entrenched in my soul. And each time I step outside my door I know the battle is still being waged.

Peace

The Pope

And

President Obama

It's been month since Pope Francis visited the United States. And in that time it has given me pause to think about the relative nature and impact of his visit in regard to where we are as a nation.

It was interesting to watch and observe the reception that the first Hispanic pope would receive in a country now torn with political rhetoric over the influx of Hispanics .

Still, the seventy-eight year old pontiff, we've come to embrace as one of the more progressive popes in modern times made his first visit to the United States and was welcomed in much the same way the Beatles were welcomed on their first visit to the United States. His visit however marked a decided change in the papacy. Arriving with an agenda that made the presidential candidates platforms look weak in comparison Pope Francis took on some of the more pressing not on the United States but the world as a whole. Global warming and climate change, immigration, the disparity between the rich and the poor, he treaty with Iran, improved relations with Cuba were just a few of the issues he chose to expound on during his brief visit.

Traveling with an entourage that included a Buddhist monk, a rabbi, an imam and others, the pope's coalition, one of inclusion could serve as an example to a much divided Washington political spectrum. His inclusivity serves as a prime example of acceptance and tolerance when it comes to religious freedom.

This is a far cry from Republican presidential candidate Ben Carson's attempt to demonize the Muslim religion with such rhetoric saying he wouldn't support a Muslim in the White House. This is obviously coming from a man who doesn't know the history of the country he would like to be commander-and-chief of. If so he should know that as short a time ago as Obama's first presidential run there were white folks saying that they would not support a Black man in the White House. But a party devoid of issues or a concrete and viable platform Republican candidates made the clear and conscience choice to be the party of divisiveness, instilling fear in those that have little more knowledge of the Judaeo-Christian doctrine on which our country was founded. Perhaps the appeal Mr. Carson has to the blue collar and Evangelicals is that of instilling fear and awakening old wounds. Divide and conquer is not a new concept. Hitler used similar tactics when he rallied the Germans by demonizing the Jews.

Leading Republican presidential candidate Donald Trump has relied on similar tactics preying on struggling blue collar Americans who fear the loss of jobs and their country to illegal Mexicans. Trump commented:

"[Mexico is] sending people that have lots of problems, and they are bringing those problems to us. They are bringing drugs, and bringing crime, and their rapists," Trump declared.

Not only are Trump's comments offensive but they are divisive in a nation that is already fractured and splintered along racial lines. Still, Trump's goal is not to be inclusive although should he become the next president he will supposedly represent all Americans of which Mexican-Americans comprise ten percent of the population.

It's funny that many of those who consider themselves evangelical Christians and many of these faith based conservatives which align themselves with the Republican Party are obviously not in touch with the followings of Jesus Christ. His whole teachings and philosophy were about the inclusion of all men.

In his letter to the Romans, Paul carried forward with the same theme: "There is therefore now no condemnation to them which are in Christ Jesus." Christianity does not carry a message of intolerance or condemnation, but a message of reconciliation and salvation.

Wwhat is even more interesting is the fact that so many Americans have rallied behind Republican rhetoric which regularly spouts fear and racism. I suppose if the Native Americans had felt similarly Trump and his supporters would have been also seen as illegal immigrants and would not have the opportunity to be running for an elected office.

Pope Francis summarily addressed the question of immigration stating simply that as the world embraced him it should not be forgotten as he too was the "sons of immigrants".

As an emissary of peace Pope Francis applauded Obama's attempts at rebuilding communication with Cuba and the Iran Nuclear Deal so hotly contested by Republicans.

Like President Obama, Pope Francis gives rise to the fact that the papacy is more than an office as it has previously been perceived but a vehicle with the ability to lead and transform millions of lives with the vision and hopes of a common home for all.

Addressing the White House crowd Pope Francis touched on a few points which may have been deemed more political than religious but the moral message that he was trying to get across seems far more important and. It is after all God's law which is comprised of a moral high ground which somehow supersedes politics.

Retribution

"For the life of me I just don't unnerstand. I ain't neva done nothin' to offend massa or the missus. I always been mindful and ain't neva been what you might call belligerent. Even when it's that time of the month I mind's my manner 'cause I know I gits right cranky so I don't know why massa don't want me to serve his guests no more."

"Ain't got nothin' to do with you chile. It's just that they got that dere pure African and she sho nuff a showpiece. No matter what you say about dem dere Africans dat dere is one beautiful gal. Most of 'em got dem big ol' lips and noses spread halfway across their face but that their gal is pert near the prettiest gal I eva laid eyes on niggra, African or white. She looks almost like a Greek goddess."

"I know you ain't talkin' bout Amola. Why she black as coal and ain't nebba combed her hair. Look at her paradin' around here with that nappy hair lookin' like she come straight outta the jungle. And besides that what you know about a Greek goddess?"

"You need to stop that mess. Amola is what they call exotic and no matter how much you try to look white white folks appreciate that African gal and can see her beauty. I believe you can too but you're just too darn jealous and hateful to admit it."

"Why Auntie Mae, I'm surprised you would even say something like that to me. How could I ever be jealous of a African? They da closest things to animals, they is— runnin' round the jungle naked as a jaybird. And she worse than mos' a dem. Why she cain't even talk."

"Amola can talk Izola. She simply chooses not to. If you had been through what that po' gal been through there's a good chance you wouldn't have no reason to speak either."

"Why you say that?"

"When Amola first arrived she arrived with her sons, twins about seven or eight years old. I have neva seen a more loving, dutiful mother. She lived for those boys and they loved her. Whenever you saw Amola you saw those boys. Times were good then. But he following year was unseasonably cold. The crops didn't come in and the bo weevils destroyed most of the cotton crop. Massa Thomas was in debt and everyday someone was stoppin' by here threatening to foreclose on the house and the land. It got so bad that he started selling off the slaves. It got so bad that he ended up selling off her boys despite her pleading with him not to.

I ain't never seen nobody beg the way that po' woman did but it won't no use. Massa sell off both them boys. Amola ain't never spoke a word again."

112

"That's all well and good and I feel for her. It must be a terrible thang to have yo' younguns just taken from you like that but what I don't unnerstand is why she don't talk no more and why massa prefer her over me."

"Maybe it's the fact that you talk too much."

"Ya goddamn right she talks too much. I got dinner guests coming in less than an hour and the table ain't even set yet."

"I's fittin' to massa," Izola said grabbing a stack of dishes and moving towards the dining room.

"Iffen I have to say another word about yo' mouth Izola I promise you I'll have the black whipped off ya and put out there with the rest of the field hands. Do you understand me nigga?"

"Yes, I understand massa."

"And where's Amola?"

"I dunno massa. I ain't seen her all day."

"She went down to the stream to clean up as you asked Massa Tom. She should be here directly." I informed him. He seemed a little more at ease after hearing this and I wondered what Amola was about to go through now at the hands of these crazy white folks. Iffen there was one thing I had come to know in my seventy eight years of being around them, doing their bidding, cooking their meals and looking after their younguns and that was that they didn't have any compassion or feeling at all when it came to niggras.

Moments later Amola came into the back door and smiled at me. I loved her like she was my very own child. I understood her. I had had a family once but they had all been sold off so I understood her grief, her sorrow, her loss and let her know at different times when we were alone. I knew she listened and heard me although she hadn't uttered in response in many a year. Still I considered her one of my closest friends.

Walking into the kitchen I informed her that massa was looking for her. She pretended she hadn't heard me but I was used to this and knew there was nothing wrong with her hearing. There were just some things she would neither address or pay heed to. Fact remained that she had nothing to say, could care less what white folks thought or would do to her. She was proud, almost too proud for her own good. She was African and she loved the fact that she was. And no matter what white folks had in America she considered herself richer because she was African.

One day walking with her sons she sat next to me and we just started talking and I asked her. I said 'Amola you miss the old country don't don't you?' And she replied, 'Very much so Auntie Mae. I miss the beauty of Africa, I miss my family, I miss my mother and father but most of all I miss my freedom. If it weren't for my boys I don't know what I'd do'.

"That was the only thing that gal had to live for, the only thing she had to keep her going and when they took them away she gave up. White folks call it a nervous breakdown. I don't know what I would have done but I give her a lot of credit for being able to just keep going. And if she has nothing else to say and wants to live out the rest of days in silence I guess she has a right to."

"I hear you Auntie Mae but it just seems so unfair. In the year I've been here I've done pretty much everything massa has ast of me. And when he comes a callin' in the wee hours of the morning I accommodates him in every way. Now here I is walkin' round wit' his baby," she said rubbing her stomach. "And he acts like he don't know me and chooses her ova me. How's I supposed ta feel. Maybe when da baby comes he'll feel a might different. He gonna be da cutest thing bein' half white and all with good hair. You just watch and see. Massa gonna love me again. You just watch and see."

"Iffen I was you I'd be prayin' the whole time."

"Prayin' for what Auntie Mae?"

"Prayin' that Missy Anne don't get wind of whose baby it is and have you put out in the fields. And then prayin' that massa don't up and sell yo' baby like they sold Amola's boys. White folks has some mighty strange ways."

"Oh massa wouldn't do that to me auntie. You ain't around when he lyin' there with me after he come real good and I's done took everything he has to offer. That's why I know he could neva do nothin' like that to me."

"Uh huh…"

"Izola! Izola!"

"Yes massa," the young woman said as she hurried to see what her master wanted.

"I'm tired of saying the same thing ova and ova," he said slapping her hard. "Now get this table set now or there will be more where that came from. You hear?"

"Yes massa," Izola replied her tan face turning crimson red and her eye watering and stinging from the slap.

"Betcha neva thought massa would do that either 'cause you takes everything he gots ta offer and accommodates him in every way. Ain't that wahatcha just told me?"

Izola who was steal smarting from the fact that her beloved master had struck her rushed to finish the table setting. When she was finished she sat in the corner on the sack of flour and dropped her head.

"It's my fault. I shouldn't have been in here jawing with you. I shoulda had that table set. I didn't mean to make massa strike me. I just knows he feels horrible that he put his hands on me. You watch. He gonna apologize to me when he ain't so darned stressed about this here dinner party. He sayed a lot of very important mens gonna be here to talk ova some very important business and everything gotta be just right. He just stressed that's all."

"Who you tryna convince Izola? Me or yourself?"

"Oh auntie!"

"Izola! Izola!"

"Probably calling you to apologize now," I said smiling.

"Yes massa."

"Tell Buck to stand by. They should be arriving any minute."

"Yassuh."

"Auntie Mae is dinner ready to be served?"

"Yassuh. Just waiting on you to say the word."

"Good. Good. And where's Amola?"

"She right outside suh."

"Well, you tell he to bring her black ass in here and be ready to greet and serve drinks when these gentlemen arrive."

"Yassuh. I'll tell her now."

"And tell Josh to bring the carriage around for missy."

"Oh, missy's not staying for dinner?"

"No. She's spending the weekend with her sister over in Crawford County. Goddamn you are one nosy ol' nigga," massa chuckled. "Jes you have the food ready and stay outta white folks affairs you meddlesome old woman."

"Yassuh massa suh."

Amola walked in looking like an African queen. A daisy adorned her close cropped hair and the long flowing yellow floral dress accentuated her tall brown frame. Her clear smooth ebony skin was like a deep rich mahogany and her teeth were white as ivory. She was truly a stunning sight.

Hugging her I whispered to her.

"Massa's been looking for you."

Amola rolled her eyes in disgust and sat down at the kitchen table.

"Amola. Massa wants you," Izola said as she entered the kitchen. "He's in the parlor."

Amola made no move to acknowledge and Izola shrugged and went on about something or another.

"Auntie Mae did you get Amola as I asked?"

"Oh there you are. Izola didn't I tell you to tell her I wanted to see her. My God I don't know why I even bother to keep you around. You are utterly worthless. My goodness! Don't we look especially nice. My guests will be so pleased. You'll be like eye candy to them. Oh, it should be a night for the ages. Come with me Amola so I can show you what I need you to do."

Amola took her time getting up and following Massa John into the next room.

"Now you know ifffen I acted like that massa would have whooped my tail if I took my sweet ass time when he called me but he tolerates her belligerence. And she

119

walkin' round here all high-falutin' like she some queen or like she the woman of the house. Missy Anne don't even act as uppity as that African jungle bunny."

"That's 'cause missy ain't nothin' but po' Georgia white trash and Amola is African and regal and proud if you haven't noticed."

"Yeah and all that regalness gonna get her ass whipped."

"Whipped her every other day 'til I thought they was gonna kill her tryin' to get her to speak after they sold her boys. Not only wouldn't she speak she wouldn't utter a sound the whole time they was whipping her. They must have whipped her for two weeks straight and to this day I ain't neva seen her shed a tear or cry out. Not once."

"That's scary."

"So, you see she has nothin' to fear and massa knows he's done the worst thing he can do to her and it had no affect so he has no choice but to tolerate her."The party went on as promised. Six of the most prominent southern white men in the county were gathered to discuss the changing face of the South since the war. A sizeable chunk of the labor force were headed North and what remained was in shambles but there was money and opportunity that loomed large in reconstruction and despite the war those that had had money still rested easily.

There was talk of reconstruction and rebuilding. There was talk of a new South where cotton was no longer king. These were men of foresight and vision and they spoke

120

of rebuilding the infrastructure and what it would cost the very same government that had laid waste to the cities and towns and what it would cost to rebuild it. They stood to make a small fortune. That was the talk at dinner.

After dinner they gathered in master's library to enjoy a good cigar and a friendly game of poker while Amola moved amongst them refilling their glasses as she saw fit.

"Well, John I think that's about it for me. I think I'm into you for about twelve hundred if my math is right. You are getting better though. Last time we got together I think I clipped you for about two thousand."

"A gentleman never gloats," massa said raising his glass to toast the victor.

"I apologize John. Must be the brandy talking. But I'll tell you what I'll squash the twelve hundred if you give me that fine young specimen who's been serving us tonight."

"Wish I could Harry but Amola's worth a good deal more than that to me around here."

"I bet she is. She is certainly one fine heifer. Tell you what you keep her and keep the money and just let me have a couple go rounds with her. Nothing more than a poke or two is all I ask. You'd like that wouldn't you honey?"

121

"You won't get an answer out of that one Harry. She's mute."

"Even better. There are many a day I wish the missus was mute. But back to this one, she can scream can't she?"

"That's doubtful as well. Had her whipped some time ago. Never let out a peep."

"Well, we'll just have to see about that. With your permission John?"

"By all means. Go ahead with Mr. Jensen Amola."

"Oh by the way, she is clean isn't she John?"

"To the best of my recollection. Haven't known her to be with anyone and I've owned her what close to six years now. The other niggras stay clear of her like she's got some of demon in her. You know it goes back to all that crazy voodoo shit from Africa."

"Well, I ain't superstitious although she may very well be when I get through with her pretty black ass."

"All I ask is that you don't hurt her."

"Wouldn't think of it John."

"And do me a favor use the guest room. It's the second room on the left."

There was no resistance from Amola as she climbed the stairs behind the good white southern gentleman.

122

"Yes she is quite a beauty although a might peculiar" massa mused. "She's not like the rest of the niggras. Probably a good thing what Harry's about to do. Bring her down off her high horse a bit."

"Well, if that's the way you feel about it. I guess I'll have a poke at the ol' gal when Harry's finished."

"By all means but it's gonna cost you twelve hundred the same as Harry."

"Twelve hunnerd? This ain't New O'leans John."

"I know but it just wouldn't be fair to Harry if he paid me twelve hundred and I was to let you have a go round with the old gal for free."

"I guess you're right. Say why don't I give you three grand and let me take her outback to the guest house for the weekend?"

"What do you think this is Jim?" massa chuckled. "This here ain't no brothel but I will let you have a poke at her time permitting. Another brandy or two and I'm hitting the sack. Say to save time why don't you go grab the wench in the kitchen. She's a right nice lookin' heifer. Broke her in myself. She's well trained and there's not a pleasure she don't know how to give when it comes to pleasing a man."

"Think I'll pass. That Amola intrigues me. She's got a certain kind of air about her not like most niggra wenches. Think I might wanna try some of that."

123

"No problem my good man. Let me go grab Harry. I think he's trying to make a night of it."

"Harry! Come on man!"

Minutes later Harry Devlin came down the long spiral staircase a smile a mile wide etched on his face.

"She's something to behold. Give you eight grand for her right now John."

"Sorry ol' chum. That one's not for sale."

"And you say you've never tried her out. Well, I tell you my friend if you truly haven't you're doing yourself a disservice. I've made the rounds of some of the finest brothels in Atlanta, New Orleans and New York and that there piece of African ass is by far some of the finest I've ever had. But no matter what I did she wouldn't utter a peep. I kept slammin' it in her and saying 'Take this you African ho' and she never uttered a word. Like I said I like a wench that's vocal. If there was any drawback that was it. But like I said you name your price and I'll pay it. Like to have something like that around to help pass the time. It's a shame you're letting all that talent go to waste. Anyway, goodnight John and thanks for the hospitality."

It was the same twenty minutes later.

"I think you made a good call in holding on to that one John. She's kind of special. I'd insist on you going up and trying her out for yourself but I don't think she's in any condition. She was bruised and raw when I got there but I think she's pretty torn up now. Saw a fair amount of blood when I was leaving. Throw some salt on it and she'll be good as new within a week's time. Niggas heal faster than most animals. She's a keeper. Despite the pain she never uttered a peep. Night John."

Minutes later massa was sleep and Auntie Mae and I woke him up and sent him to bed. Aunt Mae was in a state of shock. And kept muttering to herself how white men wasn't shit or something to the like. I ignored her knowing that massa ain't mean no harm but was simply tryna entertain his guests and make sho everyone had a good time. But not auntie. All she was concerned about was that nappy headed African when the bible itself say that we are here to serve our massa. I know this because everyone Sunday massa always ends his sermon with that dere verse from the bible.

Anyways and because I love auntie so I helped her boil some water and clean that African whore up and get her to her cabin and to her bed. Auntie gave her a small dose of laudanum to help with the pain and sleep. It was a good thing the next day was Sunday 'cause it gave her an extra day to recuperate and auntie insisted on her staying in bed all day.

I don't know why she was so adamant about getting up out of the bed anyway. It won't like she had chores like the rest of us. All she did was prance around the place

125

thinking she was cuter and better than everybody else anyway. But for some reason she was all fire 'bout getting up outta that bed and no matter how much laudanum auntie give her she just refused to be still.

Right prior to our leaving auntie ast me to step outside. When I did all I heared was auntie screamin' and a hollerin' although for the life of me I couldn't figure out what she was saying. Half of it was in that African mumbo that auntie used to revert back to when she got real mad. But after all she just slammed the door and threw up her hands. The tears were just a rollin' down my ol' auntie's face though I couldn't hardly unnerstand her arguing and getting' so upset when Amola hadn't said a word.

The following day was Monday and I walked over to auntie's a might early since Missy was due back and we needed to make sure the house was cleaner than when she left so as not to hear her mouth.

We fixed breakfast as usual and called massa to come and eat while the food was still hot. When he didn't respond I went up and knocked loudly just in case he was in one of his drunken stupors. When there was no response I pushed the door open just a crack. Blood was everywhere. I shrieked out in horror and in minutes auntie was there by my side. Auntie Mae moved closer. Massa was sho nuff dead. His neck had been sliced and his genitals severed and stuffed in his mouth. He clutched his severed penis in his hand and there was a note on his blood drenched chest. It read 'This mercy killing is in response to all the compassion you've shown me and mine!

126

Hands Up! Don't Shoot!

'They shot my son! Police killed my son! He was unarmed. They shot him down in cold blood! Oh my God! They killed my son!

I don't know how many times Officer Darren Wilson shot unarmed eighteen year old Michael Brown but one time was too many. And what was the cause of the killing? The obviously misguided eighteen year old stole a box of Cigarillo cigars from a local convenience store. There is no rationale to okay stealing. However, the death penalty does seem somewhat severe for stealing forty dollars worth of cigars.

It's a funny thing about Americans. I watched as the media declares Isil a perceived threat to world peace and yet they have never set foot on American soil. They have yet to execute an African American in broad daylight in the middle of the street for stealing forty dollars worth of cigars and yet we continue our bombing of Isil strongholds.

There is no actual coverage or in depth coverage of the effects of the bombings or the collateral damage. There are no actual numbers or statistics as to how many innocent women and children are killed by these indiscriminate bombings. Yet, when Isil asks America to cease with the bombing raids and stay at home and tend to their own business in this preconceived democracy they are summarily ignored and America continues its unauthorized, unwarranted, unwanted policing of the world in the name of justice, liberty and the American way. In retaliation Isil takes American hostages puts them on camera for the entire world to see and beheads him. The outcry from white America is heard round the world.

'Outrageous!'

'Those people are barbaric.'

'They're animals.'

Americans were outraged. Americans lead the world in outrage. Yet, when an eighteen year old Blackman is gunned downed in the streets of Ferguson, Missouri there is no outrage among white America. There is not outrage because the killing of young African American males is as American as apple pie.

The law specifically states that a man suspected and accused of a crime must be afforded due process and will be afforded a jury of his peers and provided a lawyer if he cannot afford to argue his case. He also has the right to do away with an attorney of any kind and to defend himself. That is what the law states.

If that is the case then I ask you why Michael Brown the eighteen year old was not allowed to defend himself? Well, that is simple enough. He was gunned down in broad daylight in the middle of a Ferguson, Missouri street. Dead it would be as it was then quite difficult to defend himself.

A secret grand jury was held in pretense of seeking an indictment against the policeman that gunned him down. The country had seen enough to know that the officer involved shot a man fleeing. That in itself should have been enough to land an indictment against the police officer. Coupled with the fact that he was unarmed should have also given question as to if this shooting had been within the parameters of a good shooting if there is such a thing.

Here's another thought. If the officer felt threatened and his life was in danger by a man running away why then didn't he call for backup before trying to apprehend the out of control eighteen year old? Just a thought...

As one rather poignant CNN reporter stated following a night of looting and unrest in lieu of an acquittal of any wrongdoing by the officer in question so aptly put it, 'If Officer Wilson felt threatened and his life in danger why didn't he just walk away. I would have certainly dismissed the whole incident if I thought my life was threatened. I certainly would not have put my life on the line trying to apprehend a suspect over a box of cigars.' That is a logical perspective and one that must be seriously considered in lieu of the tragedy that looms before America today.

Another point of contention is the idea of a secret grand jury weighing the so-called physical evidence in direct opposition to eyewitness accounts which clearly state that Michael

Brown fled from the police officer in question. If the initial confrontation began at the officer's cruiser and seconds later Michael Brown was from all reports a hundred and fifty feet away how then did he present an eminent threat to Officer Wilson? And why did this so-called police officer feel compelled to shoot an eighteen year old multiple times not in an attempt to disable or maim him down but to kill him? Was lethal force necessary?

African Americans are not surprised by the verdict. They realize and have since their inception into our great country that their lives do not carry the same weight or validity as those holding the guns. We are not subject and have never received the same treatment. We have never received equal justice and so we were not surprised but angrier and outraged at this latest tragedy. African Americans lead the world in outrage.

Still, we could see it coming and protested the Ferguson, Missouri's prosecuting attorney's appointment to head the grand jury. His own father was killed at the hands of an African American man and several members of his family were either in or somehow connected to law enforcement. What were the chances of his turning a blind eye to his connections to law enforcement and being impartial in the tragic shooting of this young man?

African Americans in Ferguson who had a long history with Prosecutor Bob McCullough were quite leery and protested his heading the grand jury but to no avail. When asked to recues himself from the case because of an obvious conflict of interest he adamantly refused. His objective clearly in focus he led the jury of nine whites and three Blacks to a no indictment of Officer Wilson.

And I have to wonder when recounting the events if the system with its systemic injustice has failed us as a people again. If we can agree in the inherent disparities between the two dominant cultures in America; they being Black and white then it would appear to me as President Obama has said that there is something inherently wrong when a community that is comprised of seventy percent African Americans is policed by a police force which is ninety four percent white. It is also somewhat disconcerting that Michael Brown, an eighteen year old African American male was absent in his defense. More importantly the jury of his supposed peers was seventy-five percent white. Is this reflective of a jury of Michael Brown's peers or the community of Ferguson? I think not.

The subsequent anger which resulted in the burning and looting and the recurrent shouts of 'No Justice No Peace' reverberated after the verdict and soon swept to other major cities.

And once again America is outraged. The truth is we are caught in the inherent throes of a racist society where white law enforcement feels the right to police us in our own neighborhoods like the Gestapo in Germany's ghettoes with little or no concern for the inhabitants and where Black lives continue to be expendable.

The Making of a Free Man

"I guess you're wondering why I summoned some of the most fervent abolitionists here today to this summit. This meeting's objective focuses on eradicating this peculiar institution and blight on democracy we've all come to know as slavery.

I would assume that by this time it is pretty apparent that when we took up arms and were readily accepted by the Patriots that we believed that our efforts to help them gain their independence would in turn lead to our own independence.

The British and Dutch who brought us over here in bondage and servitude and who treated the colonists with the same utter disregard for their liberties are also the ones at fault and to blame for our present condition. That is why many of us picked up arms and joined the rebellion. And now that it is over and the revolution has commenced with America gaining its independence we find ourselves no better off than when the Dutch brought us here in bondage.

Our first president was a slaveholder and was adamant when it came to not renouncing slavery. Thomas Jefferson, our second president who penned the declaration and made the pronouncement that all men are created equal is not only a slaveholder but in fact said that Blacks are inferior intellectually and these very same founding fathers have made slavery a part of the constitution that governs this new Republic."

"Thank you Ms. Truth and I strongly agree with all that you have stated but/and I would like to add that there is a larger law that governs this new Republic and it is God's universal law. The planter can proselytize saying, 'Servants be obedient to them that are your masters. Obey them that are your old and young master. If you disobey your earthly master you offend your heavenly master. You must obey God's commandments.'

They say this to us with no moral compass or moral turpitude and yet is that not why they threw off the yoke of oppression and tyranny that Great Britain had them so bound to. 'Taxation without representation is tyranny was one of the slogans they chanted.' Yet, I would be grateful if they at least taxed us in essence letting us know that we are at least recognized as people instead of simply classifying and acknowledging us as being no more than a hog or a cow, property, chattel to be used but having no other worth thereof more than a tool or a piece of livestock." Mr. Smalls stated.

"Hear, hear brother. No words spoken have been truer. But lest we be honest in our depiction when it comes to the position we find ourselves in. It was not General Washington that came to us soliciting our aid against the British. Matter-of-fact it should be noted contrary to the fact that it was General Washington who declined your help letting you know in no uncertain terms that he did not want you for his army. If I recall correctly it was General Washington who made it quite plain that he did not want free Negroes or slaves to fight on behalf of the Patriots." stated Mr. Brown rather emphatically.

"To the contrary it was the British who stated that they would free any colored slave who served one year in the British army as I recall. And was it not the British who freed so many thousands of us colored slaves from manumission and set up colonies for them in both Nova Scotia and Liberia? Yes, I do believe it was but were we prone to go with the British? No, we chose to side with those that have done nothing but cause us and our loved ones grief and hardship since we embarked on the shores of this land we call America home of the free. And what did it bring us but a government that celebrates its independence while at the same time denying us ours. This land that portrays itself as being both democratic and Christian is the same land who at the same time believes in the subjugation and dehumanization of a people based on the mere pigmentation of their skin.

I ask you brothers what kind of religion is this that believes in the cruelty and brutality of men such as us while they prosper off of the toil and labor of our people?

What kind of religion is this that condones the servitude of our people while they ravish and rape our woman at their behest?

136

What kind of religion is this that brands, maims, hangs and castrates our brethren for the most minor of infractions. Please tell me what kind of religion is this? I fear my brothers and sisters who are in attendance tonight that if this is the religion of a just and caring God then perhaps it is time to seek another religion."

"Amen to that sister Ida and I cannot agree more but in the realm of such overwhelming odds what do you suggest we do?"

"Perhaps I can answer that in brief. There is but one thing to do in reaction to this inhumane treatment and that is to 'Agitate, agitate, agitate!'

We must appeal to the moral conscious of a nation who at least symbolically believes in liberty and justice for all men. We must appeal to the very doctrine that this country was founded on and expose it to the world as being anything but civil and democratic at the same time they are fighting for their own liberty and freedom. We must expose to the world this country that screams of liberty and freedom while at the same time choosing to make us as a race, as a people forced into servitude and bondage. To that I say there is but one course of action and that is to agitate, agitate, agitate."

"Thank you Frederick. Is there anyone that may have something to add to what Mr. Douglass had to say?"

"I would like to thank my good friend Mr. Douglass for his profound and enlightening analysis of America's problem. But I unlike my friend lack his patience. Slavery is an abomination before God and as I have made quite clear a constitution that has slavery written into it I s 'a covenant with death and an agreement with the devil.' There is no sugar coating this inhumanity and I will be as harsh as truth and as uncompromising as justice in ridding our nation of this atrocity. I am therefore calling for the immediate and complete emancipation and freedom of the niggra. For those of you who are familiar with my newspaper, The Liberator and have viewed the Black List which is devoted to the barbarities of slavery you are aware of the whippings, kidnappings and lynching's then you know as I do that this must end now, immediately."

A tall man with a bushel of hair on his face stood up. His eyes piercing he was quite a distinguished gentleman in a room full of distinguished gentlemen. There was something however that set him apart. Perhaps it was the chilling air and no-nonsense countenance but a hush fell over the crowd as the tall white man took the podium.

"Many of you may know of me from my anti-slavery efforts in Bleeding Kansas where pro-slavery forces were insistent on making Kansas a slave state. Your efforts my friends to stave off this onslaught of sin and debauchery though commendable would hardly have swayed the proponents of slavery from upholding this most evil of institutions. But working in the good Lord's interest as instruments of change I along with my sons took on the Lord's work. He summoned us to Kansas to thwart any

138

attempts to further the advance of slavery. And although I admire you, my friends, in the struggle for change the time for talk ended when those ships first landed on these shores with men just like you and I shackled hand and foot. What we need today in the form of agitation is action—action. It is my belief that armed insurrection is the only way to overthrow slavery. And that is why I firmly believe that Bleeding Kansas bleeds no more and is a free state."

Mr. Douglass's, tall frame rose once again from his chair.

"Not to interrupt you my dear friend but you are aware that violence only begets violence. That too can be found in the Good book. And if you strike a violent blow that *may be* so sorely needed in this battle against this peculiar institution in the name of liberty and justice there is most certain to be a backlash lest you not forget Mr. Turner who took the same approach. He has been named posthumously a martyr, a true hero striking out in retaliation for sins against not only against his people but the evils committed against the God the Father but when all was said and done and he had made his statement how many of his people were killed for his brazen act. From all accounts four times as many innocent Blacks were lynched as he had killed in his attempt to rise up and revolt against the powers that be."

"This is true Mr. Douglass but is it not also true that his statement also sent fear and terror through the slaveholding states that here was a man that would risk and give his life to stand up for the downtrodden and the righteous. Here was a man who was willing to stand and say that it was better to stand up as a man than to lie down for anything. And how could he be wrong in doing the Lord's work?"

"Mr. Brown most of the people gathered here tonight know that I would unite with anybody to do right and nobody to do wrong but I will not bring any more hurt and pain on my people than they already have to endure. My battle is to free all of my people with as little pain and bloodshed as possible."

"And yet it has been written that there can be no true revolution without violence. The American, French and Haitian Revolutions all bear witness to that."

"Yes we can all bear witness to that Mr. Brown but these were cohesive units with a plan and there was still bloodshed."

"And I'm afraid there will have to be. But there is far too much bloodshed now. And we are no further ahead in ending this senseless barbarism. Let us at least make our pain, suffering and death be meaningful."

"This is not an easy task gentleman and there are no easy answers to this two hundred year old dilemma that has plagued our country. It is not something that happened overnight nor will it be solved overnight but today we have taken the initial steps to ending this blight that has infested America. And that blight is slavery."

Whiskey and Romance

"What's up old man? I ain't never seen you in here this much. You been in here every day this week."

"Didn't know you was countin'. And why the hell are you anyway? I thought a man had the freedom to visit the water hole of his choice. I didn't know there was a limit on how many times he frequents it as long as he has the money to cover his tab.. Thought your job was just to take my dough and serve me. But if there's a problem I'll take it down the block if for some reason I'm offending you and you don't want my hard-earned money."

"Damn man. I was just sayin' hello in my own sorta way is all."

"A simple hello will do fine."

"Goodness, man! Is it that bad?"

"You're obviously not married."

"Not yet."

143

"No. I'm not."

"And you make damn well sure you've sown your oats and travelled the seven seas seven times before you even think about it."

"Ah come on Charlie. It can't be that bad."

"It's worse than you could ever imagine."

"Wanna talk about it?"

"Hell no, I don't want to think about it or talk about it. That's why I'm here."

"That bad huh?"

"You just don't know. I walk into the house after a long trying day and am met with a steady barrage of grievances and I'm thinking. What the hell? I go to the bathroom and look in the mirror to see if I have a sign hanging from me that says problems and complaints. I don't see one but the whole time I'm in there I hear her going on and on about this and that and in the whole scheme of things I'm thinking that it doesn't matter. It doesn't matter worth a hill of beans. I mean a simple, 'Hello honey. How was your day would have sufficed."

"I hear you," Champ said laughing. "Whatcha gonna have Charlie?"

"Chivas. Give me a double on the rocks."

"So, you wouldn't recommend marriage?"

"Not to my worst enemy."

"Those are some pretty strong sentiments."

"I don't know how I could make them stronger but if I could I would."

"Do you think its marriage per se or just the woman you married?"

"Both. If you ever notice it's the woman that wants to get married. In nine times out of ten cases it's the woman who is pushing for marriage and the man who's always hesitant. And for good reason too."

"What's that?"

"Well, I liken it to both jail and slavery."

"That's kinda harsh. How so?"

"Well, slavery is forced servitude with no say or opinion. You disagree with the master and you're beaten. Kinda like what goes on under my roof. She makes a request which is not really a request and if I don't act with haste then I'm beaten."

Champs laughed some more as he poured the double.

"Come on now Charlie. I think you're exaggerating a bit. Ms. G. ain't hardly beating you," he chuckled.

"You're young Champ. I can remember being a kid in elementary school. Back then I used to like to fight. I really did. After awhile I got to be really good with my hands and because I was good I won a lot of fights. But every now and then I lost and would go home with the bumps and bruises. In a day or two I'd be all healed up and ready to go again. But most of the time I won. So, I didn't mind taking a physical beating every now and then. But you can get beat up in a lot of different ways and the mental drubbing I'm taking is a whole lot worse than a physical beating any day of the week. I mean the constant harassing that comes with being married is backbreaking. And it always ends with something like 'I don't know why I married your sorry ass. You know there are a lot of men out there that would be glad to have me.' And I want to say 'well please go find them and leave me the hell alone'."

"So, why don't you say that then?"

"What?! And have World War III on my hands. Are you crazy? All she needs is another reason to go off and act the fool. No, the best way to handle her is to not say anything at all. And hope it blows over."

"So, you just suffer quietly? Is that it?"

"Basically."

"But anyway you mentioned jail? How is it like jail?" Champs said smiling.

"Well, in jail you're locked up and lose all your freedom. Ain't no difference. I'm basically locked up, all my freedoms have been taken away and I can't recall the last time I've had a visitor."

"Ah Charlie it can't be that bad. What you need to do is man up, put your foot down and let her know who wears the pants and that you're not gonna tolerate the bullshit anymore."

"I did that."

"And?"

"She divorced me."

"Well, there you go. I know you didn't fight it? So what's the problem?"

"Problem is I had moved out before she divorced me. I mean I was so desperate for some freedom and peace of mind that I took the first place available. I moved into this guy's garage. It wasn't much but like I said it gave me peace of mind. But I've known this woman all my life and so now that I was gone I had delusions of rekindling our old friendship—you know the one we had prior to our marriage—despite the advice of friends to just cut ties."

"And?"

"And there was no difference. I was still in prison, locked down. She actually came to see me and told me I wasn't to have company in my new place. And it dawned on me that she wasn't paying not nary bill and she couldn't dictate who or what I did anymore."

"I hear you Charlie. You just gotta throw the shackles off."

"And I did. I was just starting to enjoy my new found freedom when she hit me with another bombshell. She thought she wanted to start dating again. Well, you know how men are when they hear something like that. And my first thought was she was going to give someone access to my stash. At first I was a little perturbed but over the last few years I've learned to keep my thoughts to myself until I have a chance to think about the bigger picture. And though it was hard for me to give her up and let her date with no argument or opinion I realized that this allowed me to do the same. And she couldn't get angry. This after all, was her decision. Funny thing was though that when she called me to tell me that there was no intimacy or emotion involved I knew she was doing little more than trying to convince me that there were some rules to this shit. I don't know what her rules were and didn't care. What I did know was that I wrote the manual on dating and there were no rules. You want to start seeing other people then your or my interactions with that person was nobody's business but mine and the other person involved. And I was good at it. And so I began dating as I was instructed to do."

"So, where are you two now?"

"Well, I'm fine. I date every now and then—you know—when the need hits me and I'm cool with that. And well she's talking marriage again…"

"And how do you feel about that?"

"Well, let me answer that like this. Have you ever seen an escaped slave run back to the master 'cause he missed him?"

The Middle Passage

"Hey Shay! How you been? I haven't heard from you in a month of Sundays. How have you been doing?"

"I'm good, Monique. You know I just started with Deuterman & Karney."

"You know I totally forgot. I didn't know what happened to you. I heard you talking about it but it totally slipped my mind. You told me you were considering taking the position but I didn't know you took it. So how do you like it so far?"

"I love it. Right now it's all a little overwhelming. I'm in the office by eight and don't get home until somewhere around nine, nine-thirty. But I don't mind. Right now I'm just sort of familiarizing myself with the way they do things. Like I said it's all a little overwhelming."

"Well, don't be discouraged. I know you Shay. You want everything in a day. Remember Rome wasn't built in a day. And you know what they say. All work and no play makes Johnny a dull boy. Why don't you put the job on hold for a day and come out with us tonight? I think we all miss you."

"Sounds like a plan. Let me get off this phone and see how much of this work I can clear. Either way I'll let you know."

"Love you Shay."

"Love you more."

At six o'clock that evening Shay was no closer to seeing daylight than when he'd arrived that morning. This was the career chance of a lifetime and after only three years as a criminal attorney he hadn't lost a case. So, when Deuterman & Karney came a calling it wasn't a surprise. At twenty eight he'd chosen a career he loved and was his forte. Now he was beginning to reap the benefits. He'd started at the annual lawyer's salary but in three years he'd doubled it. And took on the challenge the same way he did every other challenge in his life. His need to succeed was only overshadowed by his fear of failure. But after three straight weeks of twelve hour days he knew Monique was right. He needed to get out.

"Shay! What's up baby? Thought you fell off the edge of the earth man. Where have you been?"

"In transition. New job and all…"

"Well, you know your girl missed you. She ain't been the same without you."

Shay smiled and hugged Benny. He was home. They had all grown up together and for the most part they'd all been fair to moderately successful. Shay called it the second Harlem Renaissance.

Benny was Shay's best friend and had been since second grade when Shay came to Benny's defense when Lil Blue Boy Johnson was whipping the tar out of Benny. They'd been inseparable since. Benny had graduated and become an account for some firm downtown but soon found his heart wasn't in it and gone into real estate just when the Harlem Revitalization started grabbing several choice pieces of prime real estate were becoming available. And at Monique and Shay's suggestion he'd opened Benny's the now popular upscale bar for the preppy, professional crowd.

"Whatcha having tonight? The usual?"

"Think I'm gonna keep it light. How about a glass of wine?"

"Coming up," Benny said pointing to the far end of the bar where Monique stood surrounding by a group of well attired business.

"Hey lady," Shay said grabbing her and pulling her to him.

"Hey baby. Didn't know if you were going to make it or not."

"Not every day a guy gets asked out by a bright, beautiful, sister."

"Keep talking. I hear you."

Shay laughed.

"I missed you," Monique whispered in his ear. "I think we all missed you."

"Missed you too Moni," Shay said kissing Monique on the cheek when Benny walked up and handed Shay a glass of wine.

"You alright baby?" Benny said staring at Monique.

"Yeah, Benny. Why do you ask?"

"Cause you've been moping around ever since your boy got ghost."

"Oh, I have not," Monique said smiling her face growing redder.

"Looked to me like she was doing alright when I walked over," Shay said trying to put the young woman at ease. But Benny was not one to let up.

"Sometimes I think Mone just keeps a crowd around for comic relief. For her it's just idle banter but the brothers be dead serious."

"No, they're not. They're just looking for some good spirited conversation."

"And you certainly give them that. Had two in here earlier this week ready to go to blows because your girl here made 'em look silly."

Benny and Monique smiled thinking back two nights ago.

"I asked this Negro who he was voting for and he said he was thinking about Hillary but he definitely wasn't voting for Romney. When he said that I went to the other

154

end of the bar but Monique went on to read him the riot act then gave him a history of the Negro in the United States before telling him that she and most of the brothers and sisters in Benny's only frequented the place to engage in intelligent conversation and if he came he needed to come correct or not come at all. I mean they really got into it. When she got finished with him he drew back like he was going to swing on someone and four or five six brothers was on him."

"You don't have to tell me. Remember I used to room with her. And you don't know how many times I risked my life."

"You two need to stop," Monique said grinning as she sipped her Perrier.

"I watched my moms and my grandmother grow old gracefully and though they were both church going women they had mouths that handled things," Shay smiled. "And as they grew old there were no boundaries. They'd cut you to pieces with their words. Believe me brother you didn't want that to happen to you,"

"I hear you."

"The one commonality between the two was that age had somehow given them the right to speak freely. It was like over the years they had somehow earned the right. I think Mone here feels she has that same sort of entitlement and what can I say? She worked hard to be one of the brightest most intellectual Black woman I know and believe me I'm in touch with some of the sharpest minds you wanna know. So, why should she waste her time with some wanna be Negro. Put your time in, do your homework then ou can step to me and we can go toe-to-toe but don't step to me if you're not ready cause all you're really looking for is an intellectual beat down. You feel me?"

"You know I feel you," Benny said nodding up and down.

A tall disheveled but distinguished fellow with a large, black and gray afro and goatee approached.

"Ladies and gentlemen," he said grinning broadly.

"Gil, it's good to see you. How have you been?" Shay said grabbing the man's hand and pulling him forward in a hug.

"I'm good. Teaching an English class up at Columbia. Trying to start writing again. You know. Same ol' same ol'. Did you see he debate last night?"

"I'm still trying to figure it out," Mone said sipping from her stirrer.

"Ya gotta be careful at who and what you listen to and make sure you keep a fair amount of skepticism when you listen to both CNN and the candidates," Benny commented.

"And that's exactly why I'm still trying to figure it out. CNN was the promoter and they're obviously liberal democrats and I do think they're about promoting the most capable and viable candidate but they also have a vested interest," Mone said still sipping her drink.

"They're interest is the same interest as any other conglomerate. Money. And how do you make money? Ratings." Shay commented.

"But the whole build up, and all the publicity prior to seemed better than the debate itself if you ask me. I think I sat through the first hour in anticipation of something great about to happen. I was waiting for one of the candidates to give me the same type of hope Obama gave us when he was running. It didn't happen. Granted I got a chance to view them all and get to know them better than I had before but when it was over I still didn't know them or what they really stood for. It just seemed like a whole lot of posturing to me."

"Posturing and pandering. They were so busy not trying to step on each other's toes that they really couldn't expound on their beliefs and platforms."

"If they had any. Like I said it was a lot of posturing. Hillary as the frontrunner wasn't going to get into it with any of the other candidates. All she was trying to do was smile and look pretty and maintain her lead. She had nothing at stake and everything to lose."

That's true," Shay commented. "As we used to say back in the day, 'the competition is none'. Her only dilemma is trying to convince Americans that she is honest and trustworthy. Ol' girl is still trying to live down the scandals that went on with her husband. Bill was a mess. Remember there was Whitewater, then the whole Monica Lewinsky charade, followed by I didn't inhale. Bill was a trip."

"That is true," Gil laughed. "Bill was the man that did not. I did not have sex with that woman."

"I smoked but I did not inhale," Mone laughed. "And there's no doubt she blundered big time in the Benghazi case but over the last twenty to twenty-five years she's performed admirably in lieu of what she had to go through. She's really not the one to blame. Her husband is the one that gave the Clinton's a bad name."

"I couldn't agree more but she still comes off as cold and calculating. Everything she says and does seems cold and calculated almost contrived. I keep trying to get a feel for her but for some reason I just can't. I got a feel for Bill with all his faults and indiscretions but when it comes to Hillary I feel nothing. It may have something to do with the way she ran her last campaign against Barack."

158

"She was something there wasn't she. Both she and Bill had a take no prisoners' policy and went after Obama with everything they had didn't they?" Benny said.

"Barack was cool though. He took the high road and refused to get grimy and gully. He had a vision and a plan. Unlike Hillary it wasn't just about the power that comes with holding the highest office in the land."

"And he kicked it in the ass didn't he without so much as a bad word or scandal in the eight years he's been in office," Gil said the pride glowing.

"He embodies the whole American value system better than those that constructed it. He has returned America to what Republicans consider the good ol' days," Benny said.

"No, Benny I wouldn't say that. I think what Republicans refer to as the good ol' days is quite different. I think what Republicans refer to as the good ol' days is the pre-Civil Rights years when they were in control and segregation was rampant whenhey had an air of superiority and we were second class citizens," Shay crowed.

"Don't get it twisted my brother. We're still second class citizens." Mone interrupted.

"You're right. But I think what Barack did was a testament to the man and his character. Aside from the political successes he had he restored the dignity and pomp to the White House and the office of the presidency. Just the fact that he portrays a good strong Black man in a time when we are portrayed as anything but good strong Black man is a tribute to the man."

"Ain't that the truth. It's funny you say that. I never thought of it that way," Mone said looking into Shay's eyes.

"Why would you being a woman? Why would you concern yourself with the way the brothers are portrayed and depicted in America's eye?"

"Don't even try to play me Shay. I'm quite aware of how the brothers' are treated and stereotyped. I just hadn't really considered the role Obama's had on negating the negativity of it all."

"People don't look at Obama as a man but only as the president. But the image he portrays hasn't really been seen since the likes of King and X and it's coming at a time when we so sorely need it." Shay continued.

"So, who's his successor going to be," Mone queried.

"I have to agree with Shay. Hillary may be our only option but she doesn't really get it done for me. I think the best thing about her is the fact that Bill will advise her and will not allow her to fail. There are only a few candidates that I can remember that has

160

had such a plethora of knowledge of the office going in. Perhaps the only president in recent history that's had such an advantage is Bush and I think that he was such an egotist that he probably ignored his father's advice in lieu of making a name for himself."

"And I guess that's what makes her our only and best choice." Mone interjected.

"So, you're writing off the new kid, Bernie Sanders?" Gil said in that way of his way that kept us on our toes, cognizant and open.

"By no means. I think Bernie's got some interesting ideas and I think what is appealing to many Americans right through here is that they've watched Washington politics and the logjam that has arisen out of partisan politics and seen legislation reach an impasse at every turn in reaction to Obama being in office and their both frustrated and disappointed in their government. And I may be going out on a limb but Obama has achieved marked success despite being the first Black president and this being the most unproductive congress in the history of this country. Is there a correlation?" Benny mused.

"Bernie presents a different type of candidate. He's almost like Trump in a sense. Right now he's attracting those Americans that are fed up with Washington politics. He reminds me of Trump in that he's attracting those voters that have basically had it with a Washington that can't get anything done buthe also reminds me of Barack in a sense that he's not your typical politician. He is radical in his ideas and philosophies for the future of America. It's funny though—what is h seventy four and the oldest candidate—and he is til' the most progressive by far. Bernie's talking about things like democratic socialism and a redistribution of the wealth. His whole platform speaks of the one per cent of the population controlling ninety per cent of the country's wealth. He deems it unfair in lieu of the poverty levels among Blacks and other minorities. His thinking along these lines are radical and I can feel his passion. I like him an although he's raising millions of dollars and bringing out record numbers of crowds we as a people have no idea who he is. But the way he's exploded onto the scene by next year he promises to pose a real threat to Hillary and don't let Blacks getthe idea that he's included them by name as part of his agenda. Right now he's doing and saying things that Barack couldn't say. If you remember when Barack was campaigning we kept asking why Barack wouldn't identify with us specifically. He couldn't. By identifying us he would have been saying or looking at us as a special interest group that he was forced to defer to because of his own lineage. Instead he referred to the welfare of all Americans and I must say a lot of us felt somewhat dejected. But Bernie not being the first anything can build a platform on the poor and disenfranchised and can single us out by race and nationality and again expose the inequalities with no repercussions." Shay stated matter-of-factly.

"Let's see how that works for him. And don't get me wrong I both like and respect his candidness but he frightens the hell out of me. I remember when Bush was in office and went to the grocery store and didn't know what a scanner was and the media jumped all over him saying he was out of touch. I just wonder how in touch Bernie is coming out of an all white state like Vermont calling himself a socialist and threatening to redistribute America's wealth and to top it off by mentioning aid for poor Black folks." Gil stated.

"If you ask me that's a signature for suicide."

"But then on he other he differs from most of the other candidates because he's against gun control claiming that as American's he doesn't want to amend the Second Amendment which is a dichotomy if you ask me. With young Black males dying every day in urban areas across the country from guns how can you say you are a proponent for the plight of the poor and impoverished and scream that Black Lives Matter and yet be for the right of every American to own and carry a firearm. Seems ludicrous to me..."

163

"What scares me even more about Bernie is that he's not a student of American history. These things which he proposes is tantamount to committing political suicide. History shows us in more than one example. A prime example is Cuba. Cuba said socialism and they've been out there floating and floundering for the last fifty years." Benny said.

"And they'd still be out there if Obama hadn't tossed them a life jacket."

"So, if I may ask in closing 'cause I've gotta run who are you three going to vote for?" Gil asked as he gathered his belongings.

"To tell you the truth Professor Gil I'm not exactly sure," Benny said clearing the table.

"After this discussion I'm going to have to say the jury's still out," Mone added.

"And you Shay?"

"All I'm going to say is that Obama will be sorely be missed."

He Don't Love You

Oh, I must have known Sally Williams for close to two years when my own marriage hit the rocks. She was a client of mine and as homely as they come but she was my friend and as good a friend as they come.

I'll never forget that night. I don't even know what the fight was about but we were at each other's throats again. I didn't want another episode with the cops and Lord knows she was good at calling the police and making up some kind of charge so I simply took the car and watched as she threw my belongings out into the rain. The rain pelted my face as I looked back. I brushed the rain now mixed with tears from my face and just drove. I had no friends and nowhere to go. When I was tired of driving and still couldn't think of anywhere and out of sheer desperation I drove to Sally Williams's house.

I rang the bell and my desperation must have shown

"Ms. Williams I'm sorry to be stopping by at this time of night but my wife and I got into it and I was wondering if you could put me up until I can work things out."

She smiled and opened the door and I was too afraid. There was no doubt Sally Williams thoughts were running contrary to mine and I knew she was gathering information from another perspective and saw my marital problems as an opportunity to advance.

We talked for hours that night. At points I broke down and cried and at the end when I'd finally gained some of my composure I asked her where I was to sleep.

"You can sleep in the bed with me."

I was done. For two hours I sat and spoke of my wife who I obviously still loved dearly and she would ask me to get in bed with her. Til' this day I wonder how she came up with that one.

I obviously declined and slept on the living room couch. My home wasn't nice by any means but at least it was home. That coupled with the fact that I was out of love and this desperate old cow wanted for all intents and purposes to fuck the shit out of me. Why she got the impression that I would stoop so low as to screw her and not to sound arrogant or anything but I do have standards and this wasn't even a test. Fact of the matter was that I was a married man who treasured his wife and his marriage and was simply in a bad emotional state of mind. But believe you me. I could have been single and still would have never considered her. Like I said I have standards.

A month or two later I still found myself forced to stay with some stranger. I'd grown openly hostile to her in her own house when I realized that she did not respect me or my marriage.

One morning I woke up and was on my way to the bathroom. I had to pass her bedroom to get there and don't you know Ms. Thang had her door open and was on the prowl.

"Come here Cee."

"Yes ma'am," I said daring not to step into her bedroom.

"Come here!" she said demanding now.

I stepped a foot or so closer. It was too close. She grabbed my belt buckle and did her damndest to unbuckle it the whole time telling how good she could make me feel.

I'd grown to hate her by this point. Homeless with little or no possibilities I dug in and had even gone so far as to have been drinking one night when she tried her dumb shit.

See I've always been straight up. I have so much damn pride that if I were to get an inkling that someone somehow finds me to be offensive in any way or don't think I'm their cup of tea they don't have to worry about it. I've already left. But Sally Williams was one persistent bitch and I swore if she groped at me just one more time I was going to slap the shit out of.

Much as I loved my life I knew the only way it was ever going to work was that we separated and learned the value of the other through absence so I was determined not to go back.

One day we even called a truce and met at some hotel for the weekend. It was wonderful and I still believe to this day that absence makes the heart grow fonder. It is so much easier to take people for granted when you see them 24/7 but let one of you go out of town for a week and you'll come to the sudden realization that your mate has an inherent value.

The days went by at a snail's pace and winter had come in with a vengeance. I prayed a lot during this time. I had to. I was living something akin to a scene from Dr. Seuss and One Flew Over the Cuckoo's Nest. I was in love with a woman who didn't have any earthly idea of what love or marriage was.

I was unemployed and life couldn't seem to get any worse. I'd get up and spend my days at the library looking for work and hated the idea that I had to go back to Sally's in the evening. Not long after I started working and spent my days at work or commuting back and forth to work. I hated my days off with nowhere to go and no one to share them with but it was what it was.

I'll say one thing for Sally if nothing else. She was persistent. And what she's simply not understanding is that her constant forays into somewhere she will never go are not only useless but fairly irritating. And still it's better than returning home.

I have never seen a woman that proposes to be a minister and acts the way she does. Promiscuous was not the word. But I could never reconcile myself with the fact that she maintained she was a minister. And all the time I'm wondering what type of minister keeps liquor on the dining room windowsill in brown paper bags.

A few weeks later I was off from work and wasn't sure where I was headed if I was headed anywhere when Sally Mae approached me.

"Where you going today?"

I was shocked. The woman who always wanted me to stay close to home or who was always attempting to go with me seemed to be trying to get rid of me. Hearing this I cleaned up my little space in the living room, got dressed and sat back down.

"So, what are you doing today?" I asked curious to know why she was trying to get rid of me."

"Wallace is coming to see me," she answered perkier than I'd ever seen her.

Now I'd heard about this Wallace character before. And though I was glad she finally had a man to occupy her thoughts and her passions I was still curious as to what was about to transpire.

"You know Wallace and I have been seeing each other for more than twenty years."

This seemed odd to me since I'd been there close to six months and I rarely heard about him and never met him. And then there came the shell shocker and I knew Sally Mae Williams was both desperate and a little off.

"We see each other off and on. He has no car and lives in New Kensington. When he does come to see me it takes him more than two hours by bus."

"And he's coming to see you today?"

"Yes. He just called. He's on his way."

I knew then. I threw my laptop and cigarettes in my book bag and decided to head to the library. I hadn't been since I started working and didn't miss the old white ladies who worked there for lack of something better to do. Still, I didn't want her man

Wallace to get the wrong impression and didn't want to be there when he arrived as there was no question what her intent was. In all actuality, I felt sorry for the brother. Like I said I never met him personally but I just figured that any brother that would travel more than five minutes to see this old, homely, horny broad needed to have their head examined. I tried to draw a picture of Wallace in my mind. I couldn't.

I tried to understand Sally Mae. I couldn't. This was the same woman who only mentioned Wallace when I asked her things that were puzzling to me like why this self-proclaimed minister had a drawer full of porno movies.

"Oh, those are Wallace's. He likes to put them on when we're having sex."

Was she aware of what she'd just told me? Didn't she know or care that he was using her to masturbate in her while he fantasized about some heavenly brown goddess on the screen?

"So you two have seen each other for the better part of twenty years?" I asked still puzzled about this whole relationship.

"Off and on. Wallace has a funny way of getting ghost for months at a time when it's convenient," she said.

Isn't that a hint I thought to myself. I wanted to tell her. The brothers using you and only comes to see you when he's desperate. He has no more interest in you than a man on the moon. To him you're just a piece of ass in storage. I wanted to tell this woman who had no more knowledge of men than my two year old niece but I was her tenant and as yet she hadn't asked for a dime. This was the closest thing she'd had to a man. Who was I to dash her only chance for love and happiness?

She went on.

"Yes, we've been seeing each other on and off for about twenty years. I think the only time we really didn't see each other was when he made me mad and I stopped speaking to him."

"What happened? What did he do to you that made you stop speaking?"

"He gave me a sexually transmitted disease so I stopped speaking to him but later on he apologized."

I have to admit I was speechless. I wasn't stuck up or snobbish but I soon came to realize that there was a difference between myself and this woman. I think they call it values or a lack thereof but there is no way any of my female friends would allow themselves to be given a sexually transmitted disease and then allow the motherfucker access to her pussy again. Nope. Sorry. No way.

Now I knew without ever having met Wallace that he had no standards for the simple fact that he was sleeping with Sally Mae. This only made my perception of him worse. He'd been out there sleeping around with someone nastier than Sally Mae andthat in itself let me know that he had little or no standards.

I did not comment but finished packing my bag and told her I would see her later.

"Could you make it after three?"

I turned and waved.

I spent my day thinking about myself and Sally Mae. Who was I to be looking down my nose at her when I'd travelled six states to be with a woman who hardly wanted me?

Love was a crazy thing and the search for true love even more deceitful hiding when you wanted and needed it most. What I wouldn't have done to be in the throes of my wife's arms but here I was estranged from her, homeless and slumming it with Sally Mae. And so I struck all thoughts from my mind of what was about to transpire at the house.

Returning to the house that evening I only hoped Wallace was gone and we could return to our normal chaos. I didn't want to meet the man that would stoop to so low a level.

When I arrived home, Charles, Sallie's eleven year old grandson who lived with us stood outside, his backpack still on from school dancing. I could see he was in some discomfort.

"What's wrong man?"

"I gotta go to the bathroom and grandma won't open the door."

"Did you knock?"

"I knocked and rang the doorbell," he said exasperated jumping up and down on one leg.

"Go around to the backyard and pee. I'll call her and see where she is," I said knowing very well why she wasn't opening the door.

"Sally Charles is outside. Says he's been knocking for an hour."

"Okay give me a couple of minutes."

I hung up the phone and had a seat on the front porch and pulled out my cigarettes. A few minutes later the door open and a handsome rather well-dressed man came out followed by Sally Mae. I was shocked. Brother came over to where I was sitting, shook my hand, and introduced himself before complimenting me on my outfit. I was surprised that he was nothing like I pictured him to be. But what I really couldn't understand as to why he had come all this way to be with the likes of her. He just seemed to have too much going on to be with the likes of someone who only thought to shower every other Thursday and who changed clothes maybe once a week. I just couldn't understand but I was glad he'd come. She was happier than I'd ever seen her.

Later that evening Sally came out of the bedroom.

"Mr. B do you know what happened to my liquor that was on the dining room windowsill?"

I knew but I wasn't saying.

Where Are All the Black Folks?

Sitting on the edge of the bed last Sunday morning I listened to my wife as she went on about the prospects for her new upcoming project. Although I nodded my head supportively as any good husband would do I really had no idea what her newest project entailed. It wasn't the first time I'd listened to her impassioned ideas for creating a new business venture and since I'd yet to see any of them come to fruition I only listened to the sketchy outlines of this latest venture. Supportive yes but a betting man no.

In the whole crux of her maniacal ramblings a few things did cause me some concern though. In her half a century on this earth it surprises me how we as a people can and will so easily condemn the state of affairs of us as a people. It brings me to a quote I heard my father say on numerous occasions and I paraphrase as I too have spent half a century on this earth and have trouble recalling things that used to seem ingrained in my psyche and so commonplace. In any case it goes something like this.

'He who is not inclined to study the past is doomed to repeat it.' I believe that's close enough where you at least will get the point. In my attempts to understand racism—which I must admit—I clearly do not there is little need for me to revisit the poplar trees which Billie Holiday and numerous others have referenced when speaking of the strange fruit hanging there in the midday sun.

There is W.E.B Dubois The Souls of Black Folks who gives us a clear depiction of this peculiar institution we know as slavery and how racism evolved from it. Numerous others have spoken in rather eloquent terms of racism and it's affect on Blacks in America from Frederick Douglass to Malcolm and Martin and to a lesser degree in many instances taken on a subtler form or manifested itself in different ways than it has in the past becoming institutionalized but there it remains and many will argue that although it has lessened in degrees it remains with us nonetheless and is as American as apple pie. This can hardly be argued as statistics show in every aspect of American life that Blacks lag far behind in areas such as finances, education, growth, etc.

For too many Blacks the overt face of racism can be seen on an almost daily basis and has had a most emasculating and debilitating effect on us as a people. This past summer we witnessed two high profile killings of two unarmed Black men by law enforcement officials in New York City and Ferguson, Missouri. And although these events are not new to the Black community we are continually outraged by these events and the fact that both law enforcement agents were acquitted of any wrongdoing. What affect does this have on the Black community as a whole?

Which brings me back to my wife and her ramblings concerning her latest project and proposal which she placed her before the Wilkinsburg, Pennsylvania City Council. Wilkinsburg is a small community within the city of Pittsburgh and is predominantly

Black yet she was surprised to find that she was the only person of color at the city council meeting. I had to ask myself why it was that she was surprised to find that Blacks were not in attendance. I didn't say anything because as past history has taught me this latest project of hers would soon come to pass as all the others had before this but it made me think to ask her.

Why would Blacks be in attendance at a city council meeting? Blacks who rightfully have lost faith in this very same government which dutifully omits them from every almost avenue of forward progress and continually makes them the victim while condoning the inequality of Black folks in every aspect of American society. And she wants to why we weren't present. I wanted to ask her what world she grew up in. Did she really grow up Black in this Black man's America?

I can remember asking this very same woman, my wife, who holds a masters degree and graduated Magna Cum Laude from Dusquesne University why she expected there to be Blacks at a city council meeting. When had America ever listened and taken countenance to what they had to say other than when they were burning down the cities. We are a voiceless people so why would we even attempt to make our voices heard at a town meeting? Why I wanted to ask? But I was being the supportive husband and if at fifty after Marcus and Dubois and King and Douglass and so many others had already admonished America and raised these very same questions and answered them oh so long

ago who was I to speak now?

Sadie & Me

Far as I can remember back Sadie been there. I can remember far back as us playing hop scotch and Miss Mary Mack when we was just little girls. Well, I had pig tails anyway. Sadie's mom Miss Deidre was all the time trying to do something with Sadie's hair on account she had peas and no matter how much Miss Deidre pulled and tugged at it when it was all over and she put the last beret in it Sadie's hair always looked the same like rows and rows of peas. But she was still my girl. So, when the kids thought they were going to pick on her they not only had to deal with her they had to deal with me. I didn't much mind 'cause back in those days I was as much a tomboy as I am a woman today.

But like I said as far back as I can remember we been tight. And that's not to say it's been easy. I mean we both went though out trials and tribulations like when Miss Deidre fist husband and Sadie's daddy went to get a pack of cigarettes one day from right there at the Nigga Mart and never came back. Miss Deidre believed for the longest time that somebody robbed him an killed him and got rid of the body but more than one person has said he just found himself a younger, purtier model of Miss Deidre.

Me, personally I think Mr. Joe just got tired of peasy ol' Miss Deidre walkin' around in her housecoat and slippers all day. Matter-of-fact, the only time I see Miss Deidre change is for church on Sundays. Anyway I think that's why Sadie's daddy left that day but Sadie think it was her fault why he left. It hurt her bad too and I ain't never think she was going to recover but we would talk about it and I told her she was better off than me 'cause I ain't never seen my daddy and for whatever reason he left or got killed or whatever one thing was for sure. He loved him some baby girl. And after a few months Sadie was back to being herself again.

At night and on weekends and holidays we'd sleep over each other's house. There was a spell there that I think I stayed at her house more than I stayed at my own house. See with my momma having eleven younguns—all of us pretty close in age—I think momma was kind happy that I was gone. Leastways she never said no I couldn't go.

Now Sadie was an only child but her mother must have had ten or eleven brothers and sisters and a whole bunch of cousins and they were all close not like me and my brothers and sisters. No they were close. But Buddha was the closest. When we first started running together Buddha couldn't have been no more than six or seven and followed us everywhere. I think we were like eight or nine but wherever we went Buddha was right there nose running and always dirty but we let him come anyway. He was sort of like the puppy we never had.

Most of the time we went anywhere it was always just the three of us. When we got a little older I was glad Buddha was around. By the time he was thirteen he was a s big as any man standing close to six feet two and boy did he turn out to be a handsome boy. Even the senior girls liked Buddha. I think it was because he was the first freshman to ever start on the basketball team for Coach Thomas. But the whole idea of not starting him just because he's a freshman is crazy to me especially when he's better than everyone else in the team.

That first year Buddha took us to the state championship as a freshman and it was suddenly like we were now riding this little snotty nosed kid's coattails—like he stepped out of our shadow—and we were now in his. But he didn't change a bit and remained humble and quiet. He was just like a big ol' teddy bear you just wanted to snuggle up close to. Sometimes I really had thoughts like this but I never really entertained because Buddha and I are so close we're almost related. But there were a lot of benefits to knowing Buddha around this time.

Me and Sadie got to meet a whole lot of people we wouldn't have normally gotten to meet. But you know Sadie. It wasn't just enough that she had to meet the rest of the fellas on Buddha's basketball team. Sadie had to try them out. I'm thinking during our senior year Sadie had to have gone through at least a quarter of the upperclassmen. The whole time I'm trying to decide who I want to be my date for the senior prom Sadie's telling me who's good in bed and not. Never once did she consider what others would think and people were talking. When I asked my own mama what to make of the whole situation she simply said behaviors are learned and she sees her mama doing it so it makes it okay and normal in her eyes. And that may be so but one thing's for damned sure mama. I see you with eleven kids and still chasing after men and that's one behavior I'm going to leave right here with you mama.

In Sadie's case, it was just something I had to endure. She had come of age and when she came in to her own around sixteen or seventeen there wasn't a boy who didn't have his eyes on Sadie. And she was so well liked that she just had a hard time telling her beautiful black brothers no. They'd tell her how much they liked her and before you could say—is that right—Sadie was huddled up with the likes of Lil Joe Johnson who'd she'd just met yesterday. In those days Sadie was an honor roll student but I'd be willing to bet she was getting just as high grades in the bedroom as the classroom. Funny thing was though, the boys she slept with always respected my girl no matter how many times she threw her name in the hat for Miss Congenial.

Now don't get me wrong. I could never hate on my girl. We like sisters. Always has been and that's not to say I wasn't testing the waters at that time but the difference was you could count the boys I laid down within the four years of high school on one hand and you'd still have fingers left over whereas if you counted the guys Sadie bedded down with she'd need both her fingers and toes and mine too. Funny, she never got pregnant though and never seemed interested in having a relationship. But then if you knew Sadie you had to know she was too smart for that.

And then one day it all came to a crashing end and high school was over and we were on our way to college each of us receiving academic scholarships to a number of colleges. When it was all over we decided to stay in state and went to Hampton. When we got there Sadie received the same response she did when she was in high school and became a big hit with the boys on campus but Sadie was having none of it.

"Do you realize that we're the first generation in our families to go to college Celia?"

When I nodded yes she went on.

"This is a first for us Celia. We just gotta make good on it. We have a chance to change history. To make a statement... You know what I'm saying? No one in our family has done this. It's kind of like Booker T naming us the talented tenth. I'm thinking this is kind of what he's referring to."

I listened to Sadie without responding. She often went sideways and marched to the beat of a different drummer. Sometimes you just had to let her voice her opinion and vent.

"Don't you see we have the opportunity to do something different and unique? We have the opportunity that our folks weren't afforded to break new ground and do things for not just us and our kids but for our people. So, I suggest you and I start today in earnest at being the best we can be and change our world and our culture."

"You ain't never lied girl. And the first thing I want to change is my culture of poverty. I'm so tired of being poor I don't know what I'm going to do." I laughed.

"That's exactly what I'm talking about 'Celia. If we apply ourselves I mean really apply ourselves and climb to the top of whatever it is we aspire to be then the reward will be there waiting for us. Spiritually and financially…"

I listened to Sadie and three years later we were fighting to see who would graduate first in our class. That was our senior year when Buddha joined us on a basketball scholarship though his grades alone would have gotten him into any college in the country. But after coming up to visit us a couple of times there was no saying no. Hampton was his choice. A month or so after being on campus he was at basketball practice and collapsed on the court and died of congenital heart failure. Me, personally I think they just ran him to death but then what do I know?

This was a bad time for me and Sadie and I think if we hadn't had each other and only a couple of months of school left there's no doubt that we would have both dropped out. I had to keep telling Sadie that we made it this far...

When graduation came Miss Deidre came looking like she was going to church. She cried a lot saying 'her girls had made it' and I'd never seen a woman so proud. She was even more proud of me than she was of Sadie because she knew where I came from. She didn't have to say it but she took sole responsibility for me and my schooling and my graduation was her testimony that she'd done some good in her life. And I was even more glad that I could do this for her. After all she'd been there more than mama who had told me when I told her I received a scholarship to go to Hampton that I needed to forget such nonsense and get a job and help out around the house. But then that was mama. She had no education so she didn't value it and didn't know that it was the main road to help lift us out of poverty and the ghetto. She just didn't get it.

But despite all Miss Deidre faults she knew and was there to support just as she'd been when we were coming up as kids. We went out that day—just the three of us—and that's when she broke the news.

"You remember that internship I did last summer with the federal government mama?"

"Yes Sadie I remember."

"Well they've offered me a job working with them starting in two weeks."

"That's wonderful Sadie. Where are they going to send you?"

"I'm not sure mama. The way it looks now it could be Cape Canaveral down in Florida or D.C. but from the people I talked to chances are it's going to be D.C."

"And how in the hell are you supposed to get an apartment after just graduating from college. I sure as hell can't afford another rent. I swear them people ain't got no sense."

"Easy mama. The federal government pays for the apartment for the first six months or until you have the funds and find a place of your own whichever comes first."

"Oh really."

"Yes, so I don't have to worry about that. There are so many perks that I don't know how to say no."

"So I guess that's a done deal," I commented to no one in particular.

"And what are your plans Celia?"

"Well Baltimore is offering me a five thousand dollar bonus to come and teach. Best offer I've received and I like the Baltimore, D.C. area so it looks like me and Sadie will be sharing an apartment until I can get my own."

Miss Deidre smiled.

"I see my babies ain't babies no more. It's nice to see what fine young ladies you two have grown into. You don't know how proud of you both I am."

And I knew that she meant every word she said. I remember growing up and every day I had to stop by and show Miss Deidre my homework and if it wasn't finished I couldn't go home until it was done and she checked it. On Saturday's she would take us to the library and we'd just peruse and read and look at all kinds of fascinating things. So, I guess she more than anybody is responsible for me being the first in my family to graduate college.

She promised to come see us just as soon as soon as her schedule changed at the hospital. She was going to help us get settled in. I guess that's what good mother's did every time you changed stations in life. I think they just do this to rest their minds at ease that they did everything possible to make sure their kids got off to a good start. And she just naturally thought I was as much her child as Sadie was cause she stayed on me about everything including making good choices that you would be able to live with down the road. Of course it's often easier to give advice on life than it is to take it. And it wasn't more than a day or two after she left when we got news that Miss Deidre had been murdered at home in her house by her longtime boyfriend Tommy Rutledge. Sadie and I never liked him. I didn't like him because he lived three blocks away with his wife and seven kids and had been dropping by for as long as I can remember. I don't know exactly why Sadie hated him so but I suppose she had her reasons. We went home to see about Miss Deidre's burial and I have to admit Sadie held up better than I expected. I think I took it hardest of all. After all, no one else had ever cared about me the way Miss Deidre had not even my own mother. I can remember when her daddy left and it was months before Sadie even resembled herself but between our moving to D.C. and her starting her new job with the feds most people would never even have known that she'd just suffered a severe tragedy but I knew. How could I not know? She was the closest person in the world to me. I knew that she was hurting. I could hear her gasping through the walls as she cried herself to sleep at night. But if there's one thing I know; there's nothing you can do but be there for support. Only time will heal the hurt.

The years went by and after teaching for ten or twelve years I decided it was time for me to go and catch me a husband before I dried up and they ran out of eligible mens. When I told Sadie she fell out laughing.

"Celia you can't just get up one day and say you gonna get married. You can get up and say I want somebody to scratch my itch or I wish someone would take me to dinner and a movie. But you just can't wake up and say I'm gonna get married."

"And why can't I? You just want somebody around to serve you that's all you're looking for? I'm tired of waiting on you. It's time I got me a husband."

"*Really?* I know you're not serious. Do you know how easy it would be for me to go out and find someone to come in here and clean and handle my business for me?"

I knew what she was saying was true. By this time Sadie had received several promotions and was making six figures easily but the job kept her so busy that the best she could do was crawl in the door each night, shower and call it a night. So, I cooked, cleaned and washed clothes and took care of the daily maintenance of the house and when I came up short on a bill or car payment Sadie was always there. If she went shopping she always shopped for both of us. I really couldn't have asked for a better roommate. But a man could do things Sadie could never do for me.

"Don't you ever want to just be held in a man's arms? Don't you ever see yourself with children?"

"Yes. I can't lie. It would be nice to be held, to be loved. And to answer your second question... No, I can't see myself with a bunch of snotty nosed kids pullin' and tuggin' at my apron strings. You know I'm way too selfish to have kids. I'd have to cut into my shopping money to buy them school clothes. Nope not really feeling the whole kid approach to why you want a man."

"Well, I do."

"And I think it's healthy to feel that way but not to marry them for that. If you ask me men are loathsome, nasty creatures, two steps from a mole or groundhog in the chain of evolution. Big overgrown slugs if you ask me."

"They may be all of that but I'm hitting that time of my life."

"What time is that cause we're the same age and I didn't get the memo."

"And never will because you're married to your career."

"And my career gives me more than any man could. Like I've always told you if you strive to be the best then you'll be rewarded and I am and furthermore you are too."

"I hear you Sadie. You're at the point where your job gives you all the tangibles but it can't possible give you the intangibles like the smile from a man when he sees you in your new black evening dress. Where do you get that complimentary look and that approval that your man gives you?"

"What don't you get Celia? When that salesgirl at Ashley Stewarts puts my dress in the bag I already know. I don't need no man to validate me. And I sure don't need a man to support me. I am the new Black woman. Independent and self-sufficient."

"That you are but the one thing that you are that you refuse to admit is leery and skeptical. The most traumatic thing that happened to you growing up is your daddy who just so happened to be a man leaving who left you. You blamed yourself. And then Buddha's death felt like you were being abandoned again. And when Miss Deidre was killed by that bastard you lost total faith in the male species altogether. Admit it.The worst three things to happen to you in your life have all been at the hands of men and I don't think you've ever recovered or ever will."

"You may be right and I'm not saying that you're not but you know as well as I do that I have never depended on anyone else for anything including my happiness. In this world the only person you can really depend on is yourself. Everyone else will leave you holding the bag and asking yourself 'what the hell just happened'."

"Perhaps."

"And why should I give someone the opportunity to hurt me?"

"All that's possible but why do you think that that's *all* men? All I'm saying is that there is the distinct possible that Mr. Right is out there somewhere. But if you close the door and ignore the possibility how do you propose to find happiness?"

"I am happy sweetie pie. What you're not understanding is that I'm responsible for my own happiness and I don't need a man to complete me or make me feel whole. If I have an itch and need it scratched I can put my phone on speed dial and make that call. And when my itch is scratched then I can go back to my life until my itch needs to be scratched again."

"Okay Sadie. You know sometimes I wonder why I bother to talk to you at all. You're hopeless. I just hope one day you don't wake up regretting you don't have any family to carry on your legacy."

"I may. But I'll tell you one thing I won't do. I won't turn around in five or six years wonder why there's some man lying in my bed that I have nothing in common with and who turns my stomach every time I see him."

"And that's why you have to be thorough."

"Baby girl, I check the resume every time I consider dating one of these fools and no matter how good they appear they always turn out to be a disappointment. In all honesty men as a whole bore me. I'd rather pick up a good book or turn on Netflix pop me some good popcorn and just sit back and relax."

"So you don't think there's the possibility that there's somebody out there for you."

"I'm thinking that there very well could be if the Good Lord sees fit to put a man in my life then I'll certainly count that as a blessing. But there will be no going out there in search of. I mean really think about it Celia. Have you ever been in love?"

"C'mon you know I have."

"So, you know that when your nipples get hard when he kisses you that first day and they're still getting hot a year later that you have something special there."

"Yes Lord."

"That's a blessing. You can't go out and make that happen. You can't facilitate it. You have to allow Him to do his work. It may only happen once or twice in a lifetime but baby you can't make it happen?"

"I'd like to try."

"And you should. That's called dating but slow down and wait til he sends you that very, special, person. Trust me you'll know when he comes along."

Well, let me tell you this. I've waited forty two years and ain't seen hide nor hair of no marriage. And where is Sadie? Her old ass is outside sitting by the pool, nose in the air pretending she's reading a book. You know I was right all the time. This witch didn't want nothing more than a built in maid. It's like she always thought she was somethin' akin to royalty and had manipulated me into taking care of her like I was some indentured servant or something.

Sadie really had some issues and for the love of God I don't know how I got caught up in her life and donating part of mine to hers but here I am eighty two years old wondering where the hell my life has gone while she sits out next to the pool just as happy and content. I think she has a date tonight but it's hard to tell cause she don't get excited about anything. Never did but if you ask me if she's feeling some kind of way about the good doctor I'd have to say yes. She gets up all early just to go to the gym so she can stay firm in all the right place and I gotta admit Sadie don't look a day over fifty. If you doubt me let me tell you this. This doctor she's seeing ain't but fifty two. I know she done lied about her age and he would probably throw up in his mouth if he knew she was eighty three. But Sadie has always been a good one for lying about her age. Still, who am I to say anything? I guess she's just using her feminine wiles to secure what it is she needs. Hmph! She's still up here trying to scratch that itch at eighty. And I'

thinking that if she ain't stopped it from itching at eighty three she may want to seek

professional help. Then again come to think of it maybe that's probably why she's seeing

the doctor. He is obviously treating her. What he don't know is this is a condition she

had all her life. And he gonna be eighty before he cures her.

But what I'm so mad about is the fact that she don't mind going from man-to-

man. That's her. That's just way Sadie is. But that ain't me. Me, well I'm a one woman

man and if I hadn't listened to her chances are I would've been married with grown

children coming by now to check on me to see how I was doing. But I ain't never been

one to just go out and sleep with no man for the sake of getting my itch scratched. That I

leave to tramps and hoes and Sadie. Not saying Sadie's a hoe cause Sadie ain't selling

herself but when ain't no love or emotion connected with it well I don't know how else to

describe what it is that she be doing.

But let me tell you how I came to this conclusion. One day I left work a little

early. I think the ground beef in the spaghetti I fixed for dinner the night before was bad.

So I left work a little early and went home to lie down. When I got there there was all

this commotion and I had never heard anything like it. At first I thought we were being

robbed when I heard Sadie screaming bloody murder. I busted into her bedroom only to

find her bound hand and foot to the bedposts and her masseuse Tiny who stood about six five and three hundred and fifty pounds plowing away at her hundred and ten pound ass. He turned to look at me and smiled but to this day I don't think Sadie even knew I was there. I was so shocked I just stood there and watched. Call me a prude but in the time I was standing there I watched Tiny do things I never even knew were possible. I left to go and clear my head and try to sort out what I'd just seen. I don't know how far I walked that day. When I returned at my regular time Tiny was gone and Sadie was just as chipper and upbeat as I've ever seen her though she was walking with quite a noticeable limp.

I never mentioned that day but my whole outlook changed when it came to Sadie. Here she was the ground breaker always talking about how we as Black people should lift ourselves up and once again take the mantle and return to prominence as kings and queens and leaders not bleeders. Not a day went by where she didn't reiterate her views on this. She'd talk about how we as Black women had let America shape and define us and how we as Black women should carry ourselves with dignity and our heads held high. And here I come home sick from work one day and the only thing held high is her ass all up in the air.

Now I'm not gonna lie. With all of her problems Sadie was my idol, my hero—well—up until that point anyway.

I think that's when it became clear to me that Sadie was just as human as the rest of us. And that's when I started to reexamine our relationship and discovered the entire time I'd devoted to helping my friend become the very best that she could become I'd neglected my own hopes and dreams. And so I say this as I pack my bags at eighty three years of age. Today I start living for me. As mama used to say, 'today is the first day of the rest of my life and I think I'm going to go out there and find me a husband.

BLACK MAN

Ask me how I'm feeling? And I'll tell you I'm feeling like shit. Can't shake it either. I'm frustrated. I'm angry. Want to fuck something up right through here. No matter how hard I try I just can't seem to get it done. I was sitting in the doctor's office a couple of days ago. I'd called them at around nine a.m. that morning trying to have one of my prescriptions refilled and they told me they'd call me when the doctor had refilled it. I waited until three for them to call it and no word so I promptly put on my winter coat which did little to prevent the blustery Pittsburgh winds and snow as well as my one glove and walked over to the doctor's office to ask about the status of my prescription and was told by the old, nasty, white receptionist that it wasn't ready and if they told me they would call why didn't I just stay at home and wait for the call.

Now I've had a few doctors since I was first diagnosed with heart disease and diabetes and it has been rather easy to see which doctors have a really good bedside manner and those that were genuinely interested in my health. My last doctor had no bedside manner but was proficient in his craft and I respected him immensely. But with my changing locations it was close to a two hour commute each way in order to get to him. (Now I wonder if it wasn't worth the inconvenience). This doctor, who will rename nameless, had neither bedside manner nor my health or best interest at heart. If I told him I needed cocaine to help me with my sluggishness he would have simply asked how much and in what form. He clearly was not interested in this little Black man who he saw quarterly.

In any case, I was told that I could have a seat if I cared to wait until the doctor had a chance to get around to me. And being that my doctor has banker's hours I decided to wait. By the time he took the time to scratch off some illegible hieroglyphics I'd read everything from Ebony to Better Homes and Gardens. When I was finally called to get the prescription I was chastised like I was a six year old child instead of a fifty six year old man and former school teacher who had authored thirteen novels.

"Mr. Brown the doctor said he will not issue another prescription until you come in for another visit," the receptionist said disgustedly.

I wanted to say that the doctor's office usually notifies or sends me some type of correspondence making me aware that my quarterly visit is due. But I said nothing and she promptly scheduled me for the following week. It had been three months, one quarter exactly since I had last seen him but I know that if I had not stopped by they wouldn't have informed me of that or anything else. I was not a priority but simply just a consumer cash cow.

Walking home in the bitter Pittsburgh cold I thought about when I was a child and my doctor would stop by the house when I was sick. Those days were long gone and I wondered how long it would be before we had drive through physicals. I pulled the hood around my head to ward off the biting wind and picked up my pace. Two blocks from home two SUV's and two police cars pulled up alongside of me. I stopped immediately, well schooled in the art of subjugating myself to the powers that be.

"What's your name?

"Hezekiah Brown," I answered. I wanted to ask why but knew my place.

"Okay. You're not the person we're looking for. Person we're looking for has on a blue hoodie."

Well, the hoodie I had on was blue and white striped and so if that was the general description I guess I fit it. The unsaid description I'm sure went something like this. Black male wearing a blue hoodie… I'm sure it went on to mention approximate height and weight but the key words in the description were Black male. It could have been any Black male. After all we were all criminals. It was in our genes. That's how we were seen but and as much as I wanted to scream and shout and tear into them for having stopped me against my will I knew better. And though I had no civil rights under the conditions I was relieved. I was relieved that I had not been utterly humiliated and been frisked, thrown into the back of one of the four police vehicles and detained until they had run my record and were sure that I had not perpetrated any crime.

This could have easily taken place as it had on numerous occasions but I was adept at knowing my role as a nigga in a world I had no place being, didn't belong and was not welcomed or accepted.

I was not protesting, demonstrating or committing any crime but was simply walking home and trying to get out of the cold. But the fact that I was walking in sub-zero temperatures was an in indication that I was too poor to own a vehicle and therefore was at the mercy of white America. The fact that I was a college graduate, came from a well-to-do home, had travelled somewhat extensively never came into play. After all there was one common denominator, one prevailing factor that negated all the aforementioned. I was Black and therefore reduced to suffering all the indignities of a Jew in Nazi Germany who did not have the necessary credentials sewn to my lapel. But then I did not need the Star of David pinned to my lapel. My very hue was my defining mark.

At home I was once again angry. Torn between emotions I hated the fact that I had been stopped for wearing clothing to protect me from the elements. I was angry that my skin color was in and of itself an indictment which rendered me vulnerable to such actions by this Gestapo we call law enforcement. And to my surprise I vowed never to wear that hoodie again as if that was going to save my Black ass. And then I thought of the movie I'd just seen called Selma depicting the life of Martin Luther King Jr. Not once did I see the good reverend in anything other than a suit and tie and how many times had he been jailed not for the way he was dressed but for the color of his skin. I was angry and knew from my reading that as Frederick Douglass said the only way to overcome slavery and racism is to 'agitate, agitate, agitate'.

This I believe as I strongly believed it was important to educate, educate, educate. And in so doing we can afford young Black boys like I was the only arsenal available to those of us of limited means to combat this brutally racist society without unwittingly becoming victims of it.

I gave up teaching some years ago as well as actively fighting against racism. Oh, I still hold firm to my beliefs but simply have traded in my picket sign for a pen and a venue. Frederick Douglass' words are still firmly entrenched in my soul. And each time I step outside my door I know the battle is still being waged.

Amazon
3/7/16
17.99

30838135R00119

Made in the USA
San Bernardino, CA
25 February 2016